Scholastic World Cultures

THE INDIAN SUBCONTINENT

by Irwin Isenberg, M.A.

FOURTH EDITION

Consultant

W. NORMAN BROWN, Ph.D.

Professor Emeritus of Sanskrit and Former Chairman of
South Asia Regional Studies, University of Pennsylvania.
President, American Institute of Indian Studies.

SCHOLASTIC INC.

Titles in This Series
CANADA
CHINA
GREAT BRITAIN
THE INDIAN SUBCONTINENT
JAPAN
LATIN AMERICA
MEXICO
THE MIDDLE EAST
SOUTHEAST ASIA
THE SOVIET UNION AND EASTERN EUROPE
TROPICAL AND SOUTHERN AFRICA
WESTERN EUROPE

ISBN 0-590-34601-6

Copyright©1986, 1981,1976,1972 by Scholastic Inc.
All rights reserved.
Published by Scholastic Inc.
Printed in the U.S.A.
12 11 10 9 8 7 6 5   0/9 1

The late Irwin Isenberg was Assistant Resident Representative of the United Nations Development Program in New Delhi, India. His editorial experience included work as senior editor of the Foreign Policy Association and as an associate editor at Scholastic Magazines.

General Editor for WORLD CULTURES: Carolyn Jackson
Special Editor: Clare McHugh
Associate Editors: John Nickerson, LeRoy Hayman
Assistant Editor: Elise Bauman

Art Director and Designer: Irmgard Lochner
Art Assistant: Wilhelmina Reyinga
Photo Editor: Elnora Bode

COVER: Outlined against a marble wall of the Taj Mahal, this Indian family lends its own colorful beauty to the Indian subcontinent's most famous monument, which is also one of the world's most beautiful buildings.

THE INDIAN
SUBCONTINENT

Table of Contents

THE INDIAN SUBCONTINENT

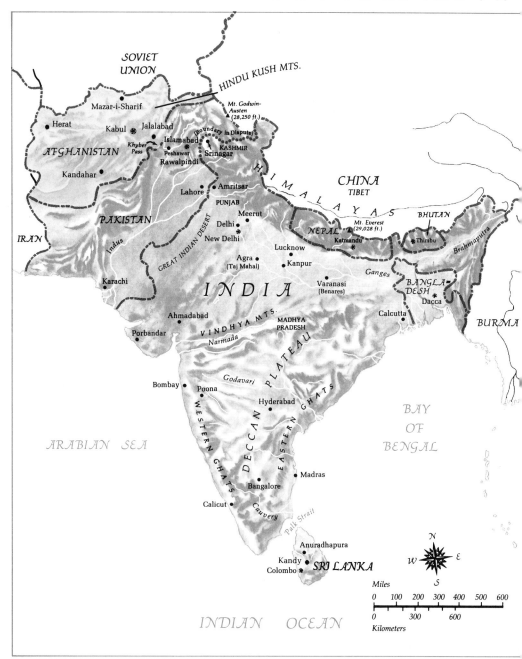

SOVIET UNION

HINDU KUSH MTS.

Mazar-i-Sharif

Herat

Kabul • Jalalabad

AFGHANISTAN

Khyber Pass

Kandahar

IRAN

Mt. Godwin-Austen (28,250 ft.)

Boundary in Dispute

Islamabad
Peshawar
Rawalpindi

KASHMIR
Srinagar

Lahore • Amritsar

PUNJAB

PAKISTAN

Meerut
Delhi
New Delhi

Indus

GREAT INDIAN DESERT

Karachi

I N D I A

Agra
(Taj Mahal)

Lucknow

Kanpur

Varanasi
(Benares)

Ganges

HIMALAYAS

CHINA
TIBET

Mt. Everest
(29,028 ft.)

NEPAL

Katmandu

BHUTAN

Thimbu

Brahmaputra

BANGLA-
DESH

Dacca

Calcutta

BURMA

Ahmadabad

VINDHYA MTS.

Narmada

MADHYA
PRADESH

Porbandar

Godavari

PLATEAU

Bombay • Poona

Hyderabad

WESTERN GHATS

DECCAN

EASTERN GHATS

ARABIAN SEA

BAY
OF
BENGAL

Madras

Bangalore

Calicut

Cauvery

Palk Strait

Anuradhapura

Kandy
Colombo

SRI LANKA

INDIAN OCEAN

N
W   E
S

Miles
0   100   200   300   400   500   600

0   300   600
Kilometers

"I refuse to think that the twin spirits of the East and the West...can never meet to make the perfect realization of truth."

HINDU POET RABINDRANATH TAGORE

PROLOGUE

A MAN AND A SUBCONTINENT

RAVI IS A MAN of 55 who lives in an Indian village of
130 houses and 750 people. The village has been
there for at least 400 years. It can be reached only by
traveling for half an hour beyond the nearest dirt road,
which itself is far from the nearest paved highway.

The village has no electricity or plumbing. But the
villagers do not consider themselves poor. Instead,

❧ "My father had 11 children but only five lived to grow up.... I was married when I was 20 and my wife 15."

---

they regard themselves as lucky because their land is fertile and well watered by irrigation canals.

Asked to tell about himself, Ravi began: "I've been a farmer here all my life. My father had 11 children, but only five lived to grow up. None of us went to school. My father didn't see how school would make us better farmers. I was married when I was 20 and my wife 15. The marriage was arranged by our parents. My wife and I had never even seen each other before our wedding.

"We had 14 children. Nine are living, and six of these are boys. Three of my sons work with me on the farm, one is in the army, and two have jobs in textile factories in a city far from here. They went to the city because they didn't like village life. These two sons visit us about once a year. They usually bring their wives and children.

"One of my farmer sons and the boy in the army are the only two who can read and write. My other sons went to school, but they've forgotten all they learned. My daughters, who had no schooling, are married and live in nearby villages. They were all married by the time they were 17.

"One of my daughters has four children; the other two have three each. All my grandchildren are in school, and the oldest talks about wanting to go to college. I don't think anyone in this village ever had any relative who went to college.

"I've never been to a big city, but I've often been to the market in a large village. It's a two-hour trip by

10

cart from here. The village stores sell almost everything you want. When my daughters were married, I bought their wedding clothes and jewelry there.

"My wife sometimes goes to the market with me. But she doesn't like to leave home, even for a day. She always says there's too much cooking or cleaning to do. Luckily, she doesn't have to work in the fields, as many other women do.

"My land used to be chopped up into 23 separate pieces. I had to walk from piece to piece to farm them. Some were as much as two miles apart. There was a reason for the land being cut up in this way. In the past, the fathers divided their land equally among their sons. After a few generations, the sons were inheriting many separate pieces of land. One man had land scattered in 40 different places. Some of his pieces were no more than 30 feet long and 15 feet wide, and they were far away from one another. Planting and harvesting was a hard job.

"About 15 years ago the people in our village voted for a new system. We redivided the land and redrew the boundaries. The result was that every man owned one piece equal in area to the land he formerly owned in scattered pieces. This was the biggest change I've ever seen in the village. It didn't come about quickly. We talked about it for two years before we voted. But I think there'll soon be other changes.

"Last year a couple of men in a village near here used a tractor and fertilizer on their fields for the first time. One of my sons went over to see how this worked. Now he says that we too must get a tractor and some fertilizer. These things will help us grow more wheat.

"I think he's right. But some people in the village say there's no reason to change our methods. They say that the land has supported us for a long time — and that changes may bring trouble. However, I think these changes will help us live better."

Ravi's story is in many ways like the life story of hundreds of millions of others who live in the region known as the Indian subcontinent. Yet that region — a distinct section of the continent of Asia — is large and varied, and many important developments are taking place. Thus, Ravi's story forms only one part of the much bigger account of the Indian subcontinent.

Another part consists of a look at the subcontinent as a whole. India, Pakistan, Afghanistan, Bangladesh, and Sri Lanka* stretch over an enormous land area. The subcontinent extends more than 2,000 miles from the towering Himalaya* and Hindu Kush Mountains in the north to the jungles and beaches of the Indian Ocean in the south. It is about 2,500 miles from the western tip of Pakistan to the eastern rim of India.

The subcontinent nations have much in common. Generally they are poor, agricultural, and except for Afghanistan, heavily populated. Sri Lanka, formerly Ceylon, has a higher standard of living than the others. India has more than 760 million people; Pakistan about 100 million; Afghanistan, 15 million; Bangladesh, 102 million; Sri Lanka, 16 million. About one fifth of the people in the world live on the subcontinent.

At their present rates of population growth, the five countries would have close to two times as many people by the year 2000 as they have now. One of their most serious problems is how to slow their population growth. If they do not, they are likely to one day outgrow their food supply.

Another problem is also linked to population. This is how to raise living standards on the subcontinent. These standards remain among the lowest in the

*See Pronunciation Guide.

The Subcontinent on the World Scene: Population & Poverty

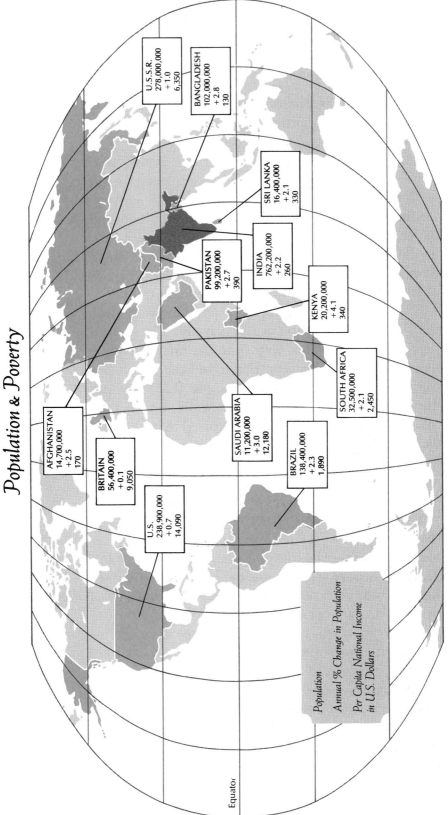

U.S.S.R.
278,000,000
+1.0
6,350

BANGLADESH
102,000,000
+2.8
130

SRI LANKA
16,400,000
+2.1
330

PAKISTAN
99,200,000
+2.7
390

INDIA
762,200,000
+2.2
260

KENYA
20,200,000
+4.1
340

SOUTH AFRICA
32,500,000
+2.1
2,450

AFGHANISTAN
14,700,000
+2.5
170

BRITAIN
56,400,000
+0.1
9,050

SAUDI ARABIA
11,200,000
+3.0
12,180

BRAZIL
138,400,000
+2.3
1,890

U.S.
238,900,000
+0.7
14,090

Population

Annual % Change in Population

Per Capita National Income
in U.S. Dollars

Equator

Source: Population Reference Bureau: 1984 World Population Data Sheet

world, despite the progress of recent years. The rapid growth in the subcontinent's population means that any increase in food production is matched by the increased number of people. So there is not much more food available for each person than before.

The subcontinent's nations share many customs, traditions, beliefs. These have grown out of thousands of years of history, and they have an important place in daily life. In fact, custom and tradition are so powerful they sometimes slow down or help halt the changes which could improve living conditions.

For example, in one region many new wells were put in to increase the water supply. These wells operated in a different way from the ones already in use. Government workers tried to tell the people how the new wells worked and to show that they produced more water than the old wells did. But the villagers were suspicious. They refused to use the new wells and even filled some with sand. Gradually, however, such attitudes are being overcome, and people are accepting new ways. But this may take generations, although the pace is quickening.

Even while sharing many customs and traditions, the five countries of the subcontinent show an astonishing degree of variety. Through more than 4,000 years of history, they have developed different religions and cultures. These differences give each country its own personality and character.

Many contrasts can be seen. Some farmers use modern methods and machinery, but most continue to plow, plant, and harvest in ways that were old when Columbus discovered America. There are great cities with populations in the millions, but about 80 per cent of the people live in rural areas. Some of these little communities have not changed much in looks and habits for generations.

In a land of grinding poverty, women as well as men must often do heavy labor. These women are hauling basketfuls of earth to a construction site where a dam is being built.

Architectural contrasts. Ornate stone temples chiseled by patient artists hundreds of years ago stand near villages of mud huts almost ready to collapse. In some cities, new high-rise buildings have gone up near ancient monuments and ruins. Modern homes lie in the shadow of old palaces once inhabited by maharajahs* rich beyond belief. Whole new cities are being

15

built with the most advanced architectural ideas, and long buried cities are being excavated and explored.

Literacy vs. ignorance. The subcontinent has fine universities and scientific institutes, but two people out of every three can neither read nor write. Tens of thousands of students have gone to Britain, the United States, and the Soviet Union to study, but hundreds of millions of villagers have never been more than a few miles from their birthplace.

West and East. Many city men wear western-type

LANGUAGES OF THE SUBCONTINENT

UZBEK
DARI PERSIAN
PASHTO
KASHMIRI
PUNJABI
URDU
RAJASTANI
HINDI
BIHARI
ASSAMESE
GUJARATI
BENGALI
ORIYA
MARATHI
TELUGU
KANNADA
TAMIL
MALAYALAM
TAMIL
SINHALESE

■ Indo-European Languages
□ Dravidian Languages
▥ Turkic Languages
-------- Provincial Boundaries

clothes, but women wear a variety of traditional garments. For most women of the subcontinent it would be unthinkable to wear a western-style dress. A few city teenagers dance together to rock music, but most young men and women have little contact with one another until they are married.

Language differences. English is spoken by educated people in all regions. This is a result of British domination of the subcontinent from the 1700's until after World War II. Most people, however, speak one of the subcontinent's 19 major languages or one of its hundreds of dialects.

People in the northern and southern parts of the relatively small island of Sri Lanka use different languages. Citizens within some of India's various states cannot understand one another when each speaks his or her local language.

Because of the subcontinent's size and diversity, no single book could discuss all aspects of life in each of the regions. Even villages just a few dozen miles apart may have different ways. Between Afghanistan in the north and Sri Lanka in the south are a wide range of living and working conditions and great differences in traditions and customs.

This book sketches only some of the major features common to the lives of large numbers of people. How do they live and work? What are their beliefs and customs? What is family and social life like? What do people think and say?

1
THE VILLAGE

Chapter 1

A World Apart

THE NATIONS OF THE SUBCONTINENT are made up of many villages — more than 700,000. They range in population from a few hundred to a few thousand. Some are near large cities, but many are specks of habitation far from a bus stop or railway station. A few villages are relatively prosperous. But most are poor beyond imagination.

Many of these villages have no electricity, plumbing, sanitation, or schools. Still rarer are libraries, doctors, dentists, paved streets, movies, or phones. Mail reaches many villages very slowly. Few newspapers, magazines, or books reach them at all. Strangers rarely pass through. Little news from distant places filters in, even though nearly every village has at least one transistor radio.

Apart from holidays and ceremonies, village life is much the same, day in, day out. Perhaps a dancing group, a puppet show, or a magician may come to a village, especially to a large one. Once or twice a year a family may go to a fair for a day of shopping, visiting, and entertainment. Occasionally, people may go to another village to attend a wedding. In Sri Lanka the poverty is not so extreme, distances between towns are shorter, and contact is easier. There the villages do not seem so isolated.

Despite the poverty and lack of contact with the wider world, a village is actually a lively place. Early in the morning, just as the sun rises, the farmers walk to their fields. These are spread out on all sides of the village.

Village boys hurry cows, goats, and sheep out to pasture. A camel, with its load of grain bouncing at every step, moves slowly, like a ship gliding through the sea. In the south, elephants in the forests help men move logs and clear the terrain.

Many people carry bundles, ranging from large to small, on their heads rather than in their arms. A procession of men, carrying sacks of rice or bundles of straw on their heads, files past. A small boy runs along with a large stack of laundry on his head. Women and girls balance full water jugs on their heads as they walk quickly and gracefully home from the village well. The village well serves as a social center where friends meet and gossip.

During the day the main street of the village is busy. Small shops sell wheat, rice, sugar, salt, cloth. Women and children have carried bags of fruit from the family fields and placed them for sale by the side of the street. For the equivalent of several pennies, one can buy a huge apple, a juicy mango, a papaya (which tastes like a soft cantaloupe), or an opened coconut. In the southern part of the subcontinent, nothing seems more refreshing on a hot day than cool coconut milk.

An Indian peasant family stands by its mud and thatch hut. In the village, homes are usually made of mud bricks, baked by the intense heat of the summer sun.

Cyclists pedal slowly along the street, weaving through knots of people. If the village is on a through road, a bus or car may drive past in a great cloud of dust. Its horn blares as it tries to make its way

⤳ It is sometimes said that the loss of a child is a great sorrow, but the loss of a bullock is a calamity.

through the slow-moving people, buffaloes, cows, dogs, and chickens in the road.

Animals are always in the village streets. Pigs grunt about, eating garbage. Goats chew on leaves and bits of vegetables dropped from carts or stalls. Cows, buffaloes, and dogs, with a scattering of men and boys, lie drowsing in the shade. In India, as Hindus pass the cows, they sometimes touch them for good luck because these animals are considered sacred.

Here and there rows of round, flattened cow dung patties lie drying in the sun or plastered on house walls. These patties are the major fuel for cooking fires. Wood is too scarce and charcoal too expensive.

The village itself is mud brown in color. Its twisting streets and lanes are formed of hard-packed earth. In larger villages the main street may be paved.

During the southwest *monsoon* (rainy season in the northern, central, and southwestern parts of India), the village becomes a swamp. The water is often ankle-deep. The southwest monsoon lasts from June to September. In southeastern India, the northeast monsoon produces the same effect in the winter months. Elsewhere, winter months are dry. During the dry season, every step kicks up a fine powder of dust. In the north, the hot winds produce sandstorms.

The outer walls of the village houses border the lanes. These walls, made of hardened, unbaked mud bricks, are cracked by the sun and pitted by the rain. Framed wooden openings, entrances to the individual

22

India's Monsoon Season

RAINFALL Nov.-April

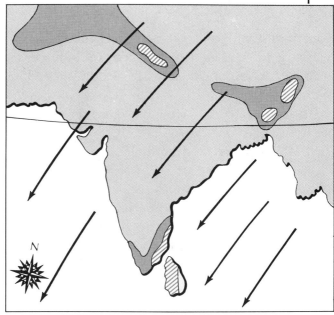

Under 10"

10"-20"

20"-40"

40"-60"

Over 60"

RAINFALL May-Oct.

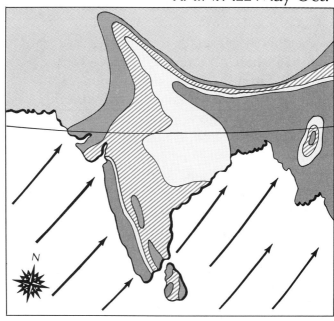

For water Indian farmers rely on rain-bearing
winds known as monsoons. Arrows on maps
show seasonal directions these storms take.

courtyards, are built at intervals along the brown walls. The homes of the rich may have carved wooden doors, and the walls around the door are painted white.

In some regions each house stands apart, but in many villages one house is built up against the next. In both northern and southern India most villages have a large pond or "tank," often with a temple built beside it. This, plus the wells, serves the community for washing, drinking, and bathing purposes.

Inside the walls is a courtyard. Some are large and shaded by trees. Most courtyards, however, are about 20 feet on each side. The courtyard rather than the house itself is the center of family activity. Here the women grind wheat, spread out rice to dry, and spin cotton. They prepare meals over an earthen stove in one corner. They spend much of their lives in the courtyard.

Neighbors gather to chat in the courtyard. Children play here all day long. Busy mothers put their older children in charge of the younger ones. A girl just nine or 10 may carry her baby brother or sister on her hip for a good part of the day. If she is not looking after a child, she is drawing water from the well, helping with the crops, cleaning the house, or preparing the next meal with her mother.

At night the family's animals are kept in the courtyard, although some villages have central compounds for all the animals. Most villagers treat buffaloes and cows almost as members of the family because the farm labor of these animals is indispensable. The animals also give milk, which the family sells or uses itself. It is sometimes said that the loss of a child is a great sorrow, but the loss of a bullock is a calamity. This is because the family may not have enough money or credit to buy another animal.

A village well is a place to exchange gossip as well as get water. Women who gather there can balance almost anything on their heads, even two heavy pots of water.

At the rear of the courtyard stands the house itself. It usually has one floor and, like the outer walls, is made of sun-dried bricks, or, if the family can afford them, of fired bricks. Some houses have a coating of white plaster. Roofs are made of wooden beams or straw-covered bamboo and sealed with a layer of clay to keep the monsoon rain out.

In Sri Lanka and southern India, roofs are slanted

25

and made of red tile. These give the village a neat and pleasant look. The houses of the poorest villagers are small tent-like layers of bamboo and straw placed over a framework of sticks.

If the family is relatively prosperous, its house has a narrow, covered veranda. Behind it are several small, dark, windowless rooms. In these rooms are clay pots or bins which hold grains such as wheat, maize (corn), or millet; vegetables such as beans; and *ghee** (or *ghi*), a butter product. Clothing and blankets are stored in chests or hung from wall pegs. Many brides receive large three-legged brass or brass-plated containers in which they keep their best clothes.

Family valuables, such as money or pieces of jewelry, are hidden in holes in the floor or walls. The hiding place is necessary because there are no banks in the villages. Some women wear all the jewelry they own. They do not want to risk leaving it in the house. Wearing their jewelry is also a way of letting others know how wealthy they are. Even if they do not wear all of it, village women are often adorned with six or eight silver bracelets on each ankle, several toe rings, arm bangles of gold or silver (or, among poorer people, of glass), a neck chain, and perhaps a gold or silver nose ring.

Many village streets are very dirty. But the people try hard to keep their homes as clean as possible. Floors are carefully swept almost every day, sometimes twice daily. The entire house is frequently gone over with a fresh coat of mud to fill cracks or repair sections that have begun to crumble. On holidays the women use a rice paste to paint designs on the walls and door. These designs are supposed to bring good fortune and to ward off evil.

During the chillier winter months in northern India

(December through February), the family sleeps on straw mats in the inner rooms. Some prefer to sleep around the fire kept burning all night in the courtyard. As the weather warms, everyone moves out-of-doors to sleep.

During the summer months, when the temperature goes up to 115 degrees during the day and does not drop much below 100 degrees at night, many villagers sleep on the roof. In much of the subcontinent, summer heat is so extreme it becomes difficult to move around during the middle of the day. The house becomes an oven, a person's body sags, and there is no way to escape the fierce heat.

The house is almost bare of furniture. Often the only piece is a lightweight woven rope cot, called a *charpoy** ("four legs"), used as a bed at night. During the day, the charpoy stands on end or serves as a lounge or chair. Two or three people can easily sit cross-legged on it.

Some families have wooden chairs, but these are not for everyday use. They are reserved for honored male guests or for the most solemn occasions. The interior rooms may also have mirrors, a small wooden table, and perhaps posters with religious themes.

Despite the poverty of most villagers, visitors are always welcome. They will be offered wooden chairs, the family's or borrowed ones, as a sign of respect.

Then the guests will be brought plates of fruit and glasses of warm buffalo milk sweetened with sugar. Later they'll be given a large meal prepared especially for them. According to custom, the women usually eat by themselves after the men have finished. In some regions, the women prepare no extra food for themselves, but eat only what the men have left.

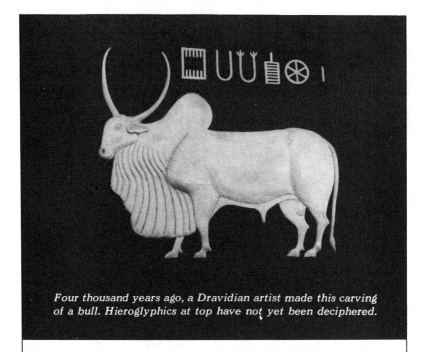

Four thousand years ago, a Dravidian artist made this carving of a bull. Hieroglyphics at top have not yet been deciphered.

IN THE BEGINNING

The first inhabitants of the Indian subcontinent thousands of years ago may have been Asians named Negritos, who lived in the forests or plains. Then, in about 3500 B.C., a wave of invaders poured in. These were the Dravidians*.

It was probably the Dravidians who launched a thriving civilization in the valley of the Indus River, now part of Pakistan. Their two big cities were Mohenjo-Daro* and Harappa*. Even though these communities flourished more than 4,000 years ago, they were modern in many ways. The main part of each city was laid out in a grid pattern with streets and avenues. Houses were made of kiln-fired bricks turned out in regular sizes. The houses had efficient drainage. Statues, pottery, and carvings adorned the rooms.

These Indus Valley people traded with other settlers in south and central Asia. And it was from central Asia that successors to this Indus civilization came. These new invaders were the Aryans*, who came south between 1500 and 1200 B.C.

The Aryans were not as advanced in the arts of living as the Indus people were. But they had horses, axes with handles, and other equipment for making war, which the Indus people did not. The Aryans spoke the Sanskrit language, which is the basic tongue for most of today's North Indian languages and dialects. They also brought with them the beginnings of the Hindu religion.

Perhaps the most significant Aryan ruler was Ashoka, who ruled in the second century B.C. He spent the early years of his reign conquering cities in order to expand his empire. After eight years, he became a Buddhist. His new faith forbade the eating of meat, opposed war, and promoted the good of the common people. Although Ashoka believed in religious tolerance, he wanted to share his new faith. He sent many missionaries abroad to peacefully convert people. In doing so, he also spread Aryan culture through other nations, including China, Burma, and Sri Lanka.

A third religion, the faith of Islam, spread from the Middle East from 711 A.D. onwards. Followers of Islam, called Moslems, began to invade India, bringing with them new customs, art, and music. They gained control of small governments but did not achieve a unified nation until the rule of Akbar (1556-1605 A.D.) Akbar managed to unite India by reconciling Hindus to Moslem domination. He married a Hindu princess, forbade the taxation of Hindus on the basis of religion, and banned forcible conversion to Islam. He believed in one god but became less and less a traditional Moslem over the years. For this he was murdered by his own son. The problem of many religions under one nationality continues to trouble India to this day.

Double-check

Review

1. Why do Hindus in India sometimes touch cows for good luck?

2. Why do many villagers on the subcontinent sleep on their roofs during the summer months?

3. What is a *charpoy* and how is it used at night?

4. Where are the Dravidians thought to have launched a civilization?

5. What did Gandhi call the Untouchables?

Discussion

1. This chapter describes some of the ways in which *where* people live influences *how* they live. Think of ways this is true for your community. Then compare your community with the information about the subcontinent in the chapter. Would it make sense to say, "Geography is destiny"? Why, or why not?

2. How are subcontinent villagers' lives different from life in your community? What would you most *enjoy* about living in a subcontinent village? What would you most *dislike?* Give reasons for your answers.

3. Some village women wear all the jewelry they own so that other people will know how wealthy they are. What is your reaction to this custom? What are some ways in which Americans display their wealth? What are status symbols? Do status symbols always grow out of or suggest wealth? What are some status symbols in your community and school?

Activities

1. A committee of students might be formed to prepare a large wall map of the Indian subcontinent for use with this and future chapters. The committee could use the map on page 6 as a guide, and then add information to it from other maps, including others in this book.

2. Twelve words in Chapter 1 are starred (*). This indicates that the words are in the Pronunciation Guide at the back of the book. A committee of students might assume primary responsibility for teaching fellow students how to pronounce these words. They could then do this in advance for all future chapters.

3. The photo essays near the center of this book contain several photos showing the diversity of land on the Indian subcontinent. You might look at these photos and mark on a map the places they show.

Skills

MAP READING

Use the maps on pages 6 and 23 and information in Chapter 1 to answer the following questions. On a separate sheet of paper, write the number of each question. Then write the letter or letters of the best answer or answers next to the number of each question.

Answers

(A) **Dacca**

(B) **Palk Strait**

(C) **Great Indian Desert**

(D) **Arabian Sea**

(E) **Indus River**

(F) **India**

(G) **1,200**

(H) **Sri Lanka**

(I) **600**

(J) **Kabul**

1. Which body of water separates Sri Lanka and India?

2. What is the capital of Bangladesh?

3. About how many miles would you travel to get from the capital of India to the Arabian Sea?

4. Which of the subcontinent countries gets the most rain between November and April?

5. Why are there probably not many villages along the border between India and Pakistan?

Chapter 2

The Everlasting Battle

IN MOST VILLAGES, the only building used for public purposes or for entertainment is the council house. Like most other buildings, it is made mainly of mud bricks. The women of the village are responsible for cleaning and maintaining the council house. But they are not allowed to spend leisure time there.

When the seasonal farm tasks ease off, men of the village gather at the council house to talk, play cards, and smoke the *hookah** — a yard-long, reed-like tobacco pipe. Each man puffs the hookah three times, no more, before passing it to his neighbor seated on the floor next to him. Village men spend hours smoking and passing the hookah, sometimes without saying a word.

The major purpose of the council house is to serve as the seat of local government. Village leaders meet here once a month to discuss issues that affect the community.

At one council meeting, for example, a long-simmering dispute over the boundaries of a piece of land was being heard. The question had come to a head because one man wanted to give the land to his son, but another family was contesting the boundary lines. The record of land boundaries, kept in the district office in a larger village 10 miles away, had been looked at, but it did not clear up the problem. After long discussion, the council worked out a compromise acceptable to both sides.

The next subject on the council's agenda involved the installation of a new well. Did the village really need the well? If so, what type should it be and where should it be dug? How should construction costs be shared?

The council's last task was to discuss the possibility of asking the district authorities to send an agricultural expert to the village. He could teach the farmers how to apply a new type of fertilizer and how to improve irrigation. When the council decided to send for such a man, the village scribe was asked to write a letter to the district officials.

At its next meeting, the council discussed how the coming wheat crop should be marketed. Until that time every family had sold its surplus wheat locally, usually for a lower price than at a large grain market 15 miles away. After long debate the council agreed to pool all surplus wheat and sell it in one lot at the grain market. The money would then be divided according to how much wheat each family had put in the pool.

Since this was so important, the council decided that its decision should be approved by the village families in a vote. The villagers were enthusiastic

◄§ The daily work routine in the villages is hard, the battle between people and nature is everlasting.

about the idea because it promised to raise their incomes considerably. The vote was held a few weeks later, winning unanimous approval.

The daily work routine in the villages is hard, the battle between people and nature is everlasting. For example, large parts of the subcontinent have little water for irrigation. The frequent droughts cause crop failures. In other places, rainfall is sometimes so heavy that large areas may be submerged. Wherever they live and whatever they grow, most farmers of the subcontinent work long and hard to eke out a living from the land.

At the start of summer farmers in the rice-growing regions watch the sky anxiously for signs of the summer monsoon. Soon black clouds build up in towering layers. Then, suddenly, they discharge their flood of water upon the parched land. As the rains end, the sowing begins. During the growing season, every member of the farm family pitches in to transplant and weed the rice plants. In the autumn the whole family works to gather the harvest. Then the rice is threshed. Soon, as part of the endless cycle of work, it is time to ready the soil for the next planting.

A novel, *Nectar in a Sieve,* by Kamala Markandaya, describes the life of an Indian farm family. Approaching her new home after her wedding, the bride sees "a mud hut, thatched, small, set near a paddy [rice field], with two or three similar huts nearby. Across the doorway is a garland of mango leaves, symbol of happiness and good fortune. Two rooms, one a sort of storehouse for grain, the rest for

35

everything else." Her husband had built all this by himself. The house and a few acres were all he had, but he was happy. Do I not have a wife, a piece of land, a house? he asks himself. What more does a man need?

In the story, life on the farm is demanding. During the harvest season, both husband and wife work from before dawn until past twilight. At the season's end, the rent for the land is paid. A small store of rice, peas, and pepper (in pods) is set aside for the months before the next harvest. The remainder of the crop is sold in the market. A bit of cloth and some sugar is bought. Finally, a few *rupees** are put aside to meet an emergency such as crop failure. (An Indian rupee is worth about 13 U.S. cents; a Pakistani or Sri Lankan rupee, a few cents less.)

In good years, says the wife in the story, "we ate well: rice for morning and evening meals; dal [a kind of lentil]; sometimes a coconut grated fine and cooked in milk and sugar; sometimes a wheatcake fried in butter and melting in the mouth." But one year the rains did not come in time, and the crops withered and died. "We fed on whatever we could find: the soft, ripe fruit of a prickly pear; a sweet potato or two, blackened and half rotten. Early and late my sons roamed the countryside, returning with a few bamboo shoots, a stick of sugar cane left on some deserted field, or a piece of coconut picked up from the gutter in the town."

The margin between scarcity and sufficiency has always been thin for most people in the subcontinent. If the rains failed or came too late, if the crops were struck by disease, if the locusts swarmed, if the seed was poor, if credit to buy supplies was unobtainable, the farmer was faced with crisis. In 1944, for example, a part of India was struck by a terrible famine

36

*When famine hit Indian state of Bihar
in 1960's, only free food sent by U.S. and other
governments kept many children from starving.*

and hundreds of thousands of people died. After two successive drought years in the 1960's, famine conditions existed once again. Only huge emergency shipments of wheat from the United States and other countries prevented large-scale starvation.

By now steps have been taken to prevent mass starvation. But even in the best of times about half of the people do not get enough to eat. The calorie intake of the average Indian or Pakistani is far below the minimum needed by the human body for good health. In one village in West Pakistan, a team of doctors found that every child had at least one disease traceable to the effects of a poor diet.

Each year tens of thousands of people in the subcontinent die of food-deficiency diseases. An estimated one fourth of all the children born in the subcontinent die before the age of five as a result of diseases caused by malnutrition. Many of the survivors never have good health and never can work at normal capacity.

Not all villagers are farmers. Some villages are near large cities, and some of the men work in factories. In the coastal areas there are many fishing villages. In the wooded areas are villages where the men are loggers. In other villages are craftsmen with specialized skills — weaving and others — developed over the centuries.

In one Pakistani village virtually all the men are carpet weavers. They are at their looms up to 12 hours a day, earning about $50 a month. This is high pay by the standards of the subcontinent. Young sons of these weavers are taken in as apprentices in the trade. Their small fingers are nimble enough to master the delicate art. The boys often work a full day by the time they are 14. As a result, they have little chance to continue school. An extra pair of

*An age-old task performed in an age-old manner.
Wheat field is irrigated with long, hollow
log which catches water from a ditch in one end.
Men walk across top of log, tilting
it and its tiny supply of water into field.
Then they walk back, tilting log back into ditch.*

hands at the loom is more immediately valuable to the family than a boy's education, which brings home no rupees right away.

☆　☆　☆　☆　☆　☆　☆　☆　☆

In India, two white bullocks, guided by a boy about 12, slowly circle a well. As the hump-backed bullocks walk, heads low and eyes unblinking, they activate a mechanism that looks like a small Ferris wheel. Its rectangular metal buckets, spaced about 10 inches apart, fill with water at the bottom of the well and move slowly to the surface. As the return trip begins, the buckets spill the water into a broad, sloping pan. The water runs from the pan into a system of shallow canals leading to each farm field in the area.

Early in the morning, the boy had walked to the field from his village home. He felt proud that his father had entrusted him with an important job. The field with peas and cauliflower was the one to be watered this day.

First he scooped away the bank of dirt in several places along the rows of vegetables. Then he dammed the canal beyond the last scoop with a wooden board jammed firmly into the earth. Now, as the bullocks do their work, the clear well water runs along the canals, through the breaks in the dirt, and into the field where needed. This is an ancient, slow method of irrigation. It may take all day to water a small field. Aside from its slowness, it is reasonably efficient and still in wide use throughout the subcontinent.

In a Pakistani field, two bullocks, guided by a white-haired old man with a face creased by a lifetime of exposure to sun, wind, and dust, are also walking in an endless circle. The animals are moving a stone grinder which is steadily squeezing the juice from long sugar-cane stalks. These were just cut by the villagers and carried from the fields in great bundles on their heads or on carts. As the carts moved to the grinder, boys ran after them to pull out stalks. The boys chewed these for the sweet juice, a favorite treat.

As the grinder squeezes, juice flows into a large jug. When the jug is full, two men pour the liquid into a cooking pan placed over a charcoal fire set in a hole in the earth. The liquid boils away and leaves great mounds of brown sugar in the pan. Allowed to cool, the mounds are shaped into loaves looking something like brown bread.

This too is an old and slow method. The men are working in the same place and in the same way as their forebears had done for endless generations. Eventually the sugar will be carted to a large village five miles away and sold at the weekly market.

In Sri Lanka, women dressed in bright-hued long skirts work on the sunny slope of a hillside amidst the deep green of a vast tea plantation. Their heads are covered with white cloths to ward off the sun. The movements of the women, as they quickly pluck two leaves and a bud at a time from the tea bushes, have a natural rhythm, as though in time to music. In one easy motion, they pick the tea leaves and throw them into large wicker baskets hung on their backs.

Some of the women are doing just what their mothers and grandmothers did, working in the same way and on the same slopes. A good worker can pick as many as 50 pounds of leaves a day, even though it takes several thousand tea leaves to make a pound. When a woman fills her basket, she carries it to a collection point. There it is emptied into a sack and taken to a tea factory for drying and sorting. Later the tea will be shipped to distant parts of the world.

As we have seen, whether in India, Pakistan, Afghanistan, Bangladesh, or Sri Lanka, much work proceeds in age-old patterns.

Alexander the Great, the first European conqueror of India, receives the surrender of the Indian prince, Porus, in 326 B.C.

EUROPE COMES TO INDIA

OVER THE THOUSANDS of years of Indian history, the subcontinent has been invaded many times. During the early centuries all the invading armies were from elsewhere in Asia, from the north and the east. In the year 326 B.C., however, the first European conqueror marched in at the head of a powerful army. He was Alexander the Great, the Greek warrior-king. He put under his command all the lands between his home country and northwest India.

Alexander swept into India by way of Iran and Afghanistan, erecting a chain of new cities as he pushed forward. Reaching the fertile plains of northwest India (today called the Punjab), he defeated the armies and the war elephants of the reigning Prince Porus. But Alexander, overextended, had trouble holding his gains. His own soldiers mutinied, and he was forced to curtail his march after having gone only a short distance into the northwest part of the subcontinent. India was the eastern limit of his conquests.

No other European leader managed to establish a firm link with India for another 18 centuries. Europeans knew of India, of course, but the overland route between the continents was exhaustingly long. Danger threatened all along the way. In the early 1400's, Portugal's Prince Henry the Navigator began sending exploration ships down the west coast of Africa. He hoped that his captains would find their way around Africa and proceed to India.

In 1498 Vasco da Gama, a Portuguese captain, circled the Cape of Good Hope at Africa's southern tip. Then he sailed north and east to India's Malabar Coast at the southern part of the subcontinent. There he dropped anchor off the port city of Calicut. Da Gama was the first European to reach India by sea. (Six years earlier, Columbus, sailing westward for India, discovered another land. Thinking he had reached his destination, he named the people he met "Indians" — one of history's greatest misnomers.)

Da Gama returned to Portugal along the same route. He bore with him a letter from a Hindu ruler to the Portuguese king, offering to set up trade between the two countries. India had spices. Portugal had gold and silver. Each was ready to do business. So the East-West traffic began.

During the 1500's, the Portuguese controlled all of

Europe's trade with India. Gradually other Europeans — the Dutch, the French, the English — began to compete. In 1600 England's Queen Elizabeth I granted a charter to "The Governor and Company of Merchants in London Trading in the East Indies." Later known as the East India Company, this private firm operated with the official approval and blessing of the English government for more than 250 years.

The East India Company soon grew beyond an ordinary trading firm. It took a strong hand in governing the Indian states and controlling their economy. It collected taxes and provided their armed forces.

Two East India Company men in the 1700's helped lead their organization to its place as an empire builder. One was Robert Clive (1725-74). Starting as a clerk, he swiftly became a statesman and commander of a large army. He set up company outposts all over India. From these he sent armed forces first against the French competitors and later against the Indians themselves. In 1757 he led an army against the troops of the Moslem *nawab** (ruler) of the Indian state of Bengal, and defeated him on the plains of Plassey, not far from the present city of Calcutta. Clive's victory at Plassey laid the foundations for the British Empire in India.

Warren Hastings (1732-1818) was the second great British empire builder in India. He also began as a teen-age clerk and rose to become governor-general of all the company's holdings. He reorganized the company's finances and administration and put them on a sound business basis. Another of his notable achievements was to defeat a combined French-Indian move to expel the company from the Indian subcontinent. Hastings solidified the company's hold on India established by Clive.

Both Clive and Hastings came to unhappy ends. Clive was accused of taking large sums of company money for his own use. He committed suicide. Hastings was tried by the British House of Lords for corruption and cruelty. He was acquitted but spent his entire fortune in his own defense.

Double-check

Review

1. What is the major purpose of the council house?

2. Why do an estimated one fourth of all the children born on the sub-continent die before the age of five?

3. Who was the first European conqueror to march into India, and what was his native country?

4. During the 1500's, what people controlled all of Europe's trade with India?

5. Which country established the East India Trading Company, and how long did the company operate in India?

Discussion

1. What roles should the United States and other developed nations play in helping poorer countries? What responsibilities, if any, does the U.S. have to subcontinent countries who might need aid? What are some advantages and disadvantages of giving aid to other countries?

2. How do you react to the photo on page 39 — do these men seem foolish to you for irrigating this way, or do they seem smart and clever for having figured out a way to irrigate without modern technology? Do you think American farmers would be willing to irrigate this way? Why, or why not?

3. How can child labor benefit a society? How might it harm a society in the long run? What effects do you think having to work a full day by the time a person is 14 might have on a young person? How might it change someone's life — now and in the future?

Activities

1. Some students might attend a meeting of a local governing body and report to the class on what items were discussed and on how the deliberations compared with those of the village council described in this chapter.

2. Some students might write a short story or an imaginary newspaper article about the children in the photograph on page 34 that would describe an event in the children's lives.

3. Other students might research and report to the rest of the class on the origins of the names *India, Pakistan, Afghanistan, Bangladesh,* and *Sri Lanka.*

Skills

WHEAT PRODUCTION IN INDIA 1966-1982

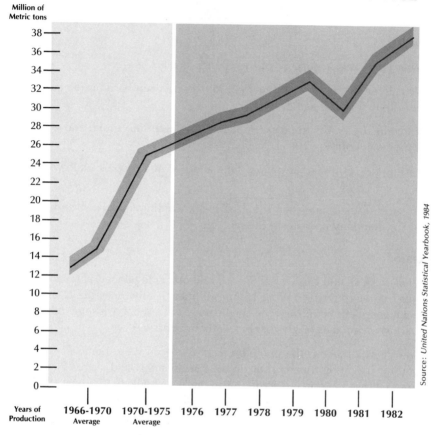

Million of Metric tons

Source: United Nations Statistical Yearbook, 1984

Use the line graph above and information in Chapter 2 to answer the following questions.

1. What do the numbers on the bottom of the graph represent?
(a) tons of wheat   (b) years of production   (c) numbers of farmers

2. How many years does the information in this graph cover?
(a) 17   (b) 10   (c) 78

3. In what year was the greatest decrease in production?
(a) 1977   (b) 1979   (c) 1980

4. How much wheat was produced in 1976?
(a) 28.5 metric tons   (b) 21.8 metric tons   (c) 28.5 million metric tons

5. In what year was a drought least likely to have happened?
(a) 1980   (b) 1976   (c) 1982

Chapter 3

Education and Progress

SINCE THE 1950's, the nations of the subcontinent have put great emphasis on education in an effort to provide their people with skills to use in a changing world. More young people are now in school than ever before. But many tens of millions still do not attend. In India alone, according to a government estimate, at least 90 million school-age children under 15 do not go to school. Many of them have never attended for even a day.

Luxmi is an intelligent, pretty 14-year-old girl from a village of 5,000 people in the Indian state of West Bengal. She has never been to school. Nor has she thought much about going. She is not even quite sure if there is a school in her village. Anyway, as she puts it, her own lack of schooling doesn't really matter. What is important, she believes, is that her mother has taught her all she will need to know when she becomes a wife and mother herself.

*Despite great poverty, education is on the march.
Above, an open-air school in Pakistan — not
very comfortable, but better than nothing.*

Ali is the only teacher in a small Bangladesh
village. He is dedicated to his job and eager to teach.
But, as he himself admits, he is handicapped because
he has only a high school diploma. His schoolhouse is
an old one-room building. Most of the time he teaches
outdoors under the shade of a tree. There are 43
students in his class, ranging in age from seven to 11.

48

Somehow he must teach them all at the same time. He must get along without a blackboard or chalk, without books, pencils, or paper. When he wants to write he does so in the sand with a stick. He knows that all this is unsatisfactory, but he does the best he can.

Most village schoolrooms in the subcontinent are overcrowded. Like Ali, many teachers have not had enough training. Books, even when available, are sometimes so scarce that they must be locked up at night and, therefore, cannot be taken home by the students. Many of the books are ready to fall apart.

In Sri Lanka, school facilities are better than in India and Pakistan. Almost every village has its own neat, small schoolhouse. The Sri Lankan government and village leaders make great efforts to see that all young people go to school. As a result, that nation enjoys one of the highest literacy rates in Asia.

Despite the great poverty, the slowness of change, and the lack of good education opportunities, there has been much progress in the villages in recent years. Some changes may seem modest to an outsider, but they actually amount to a revolution in the village way of life.

A former resident, returning to his village after an absence of 20 years, noted many improvements. The number of sugar presses had increased from two to nine. The number of wooden plows used by farmers had increased from 62 to more than a hundred. In addition, many village families were now using metal plows.

One piece of equipment that had become popular was the fodder cutter. Years ago someone in the family had to spend an hour or two daily chopping fodder for the animals. Now, many families in the village owned hand-operated mechanical cutters

✥ Despite the great poverty, the slowness of change, and the lack of good education opportunities, there has been much progress in the villages in recent years.

---

which did the same work with less effort in a third of the time. Probably more change has occurred in this village in the past 20 years than in the previous thousand.

One village in the Indian state of Madhya Pradesh* in central India is typical of many progressive hamlets in the subcontinent. Most of the 200 families living in the village are farm families. Five years ago, the village had no electricity. Now it has electricity which brings power to six motor-driven well pumps and to light the tiny main street — but not yet to any of the houses.

The village has a small health center run by a nurse who attends to minor illnesses. A doctor visits once every two weeks. A dentist comes every six months for three or four days. The village has a youth club. In addition, it is the center of a government-sponsored animal-health program which aims to produce healthier cows with greater milk production. The villagers hope eventually to sell their milk to a distributor who will truck it to a city dairy plant. If this happens, they should benefit by an increase in income.

The villagers voluntarily helped build a paved road in the area. Now they are planning an addition to the schoolhouse, which will let all children in the village, who now go to school for at least four years, extend their schooling to six years. After the last year,

Bengalis called the Damodar "River of Sorrows"
for its annual flooding which brought pestilence
and famine. Now dams control flooding, bring
irrigation, and provide electric power.

the children will be encouraged to continue school in
a nearby town.

A fishing village in Sri Lanka has also recently
experienced a revolutionary change. Until a few
years ago, the village fishermen went out to sea daily

51

in their canoes and log boats just as their ancestors had. Now they have fitted their boats with small motors. They travel to richer fishing grounds and follow the moving schools of fish. As a result, the daily catch has nearly doubled in the past few years. The fishermen have built a small ice plant to store the catch and a stall where people may buy fish. Some of the catch is sold to exporters. As these seemingly small changes are multiplied, they will enable more rapid progress to take place in the years to come.

Some of the biggest changes have occurred in the Punjab,* one of the subcontinent's richer areas. There a "green revolution" is taking place. Fields are being planted with a strong, disease-resistant, fast-growing type of wheat. Farmers are being trained at government centers to grow this wheat. Chemical fertilizer is being used in large quantities. Many more miles of irrigation canals have been dug. All this has resulted in large crop increases.

Tractors and other modern farm machines are in use. Small brick houses are replacing mud homes. Electricity is being brought to the countryside. New schools have been built and school attendance has shot up. Richer farmers even have Indian-made cars, and a number of people now own motor scooters.

In one village, crop yields have tripled in the last 15 years. The major reason for the increase is the new irrigation pumps. These have allowed the farmers to have three planting seasons a year instead of the two they formerly had.

"I have 25 acres of land," one young farmer of the area says. "I plant most of my land in sugar cane and wheat. The rest is in potatoes, carrots, onions, peas, and a bit of cotton. Two of my brothers, two laborers who have been working for my family for 30 years, and I do all the farm work.

"Five years ago we used a mechanical cutter for the first time. Last year one of my neighbors bought a tractor. I paid him to use it on my fields after he finished his own. This year I am planting the new type of wheat which is supposed to produce many times as much as the old kind. One of my brothers has gone to a government demonstration farm to learn all about planting and cultivating it. Next year we hope to get a better type of well pump for the fields."

This "green revolution" is being promoted on many fronts. Siddhartha is a crop expert. The government pays him to advise the farmers of 10 villages on the best possible management and use of their soil. Ajoy is a scientist in a government laboratory. He is trying to discover better ways to fight plant diseases. Indrajit is a teacher in an agricultural college where students are learning modern farming methods. Atal is a student in that college, determined to farm the family land with the most scientific techniques.

All this is just a beginning. The "green revolution" has reached only a small number of farming communities. Though many important changes have occurred in the villages, life in most of them remains much as it has always been. The villages still form a world apart.

Double-check

Review

1. Since the 1950's, why have the nations of the subcontinent put great emphasis on education?

2. In India, approximately how many school-age children under 15 do not go to school?

3. How much academic training does Ali have?

4. Which subcontinent nation has one of the highest literacy rates in Asia?

5. What are three benefits provided by dams on the Damodar River?

Discussion

1. Is a school with one teacher for all the grades necessarily a bad school? What might be some advantages and disadvantages of such a school? Give reasons to support your answers.

2. This chapter points out that the Sri Lankan government and village leaders make great efforts to be sure that *all* young people go to school. Do you think that governments and local leaders should do this in *all* countries? Why, or why not?

3. Can change come too fast in some countries? Can change ever be too slow? What changes have come to *your* community in the last few years? Do you think most of the changes were for better, or for worse? Why? If you went away for 20 years, what changes might you find on your return?

Activities

1. Some students might role-play a discussion between Ali and Luxmi — with Luxmi insisting that she has learned all she needs to know in life from her mother, and Ali trying to convince her of the importance of getting a formal education.

2. A farmer or a government agricultural expert might be invited to class to discuss changes in agriculture in the last 25 years.

3. A committee of students might research and report on the current status of the "green revolution" on the Indian subcontinent.

54

Skills

LITERACY RATES IN EIGHT COUNTRIES

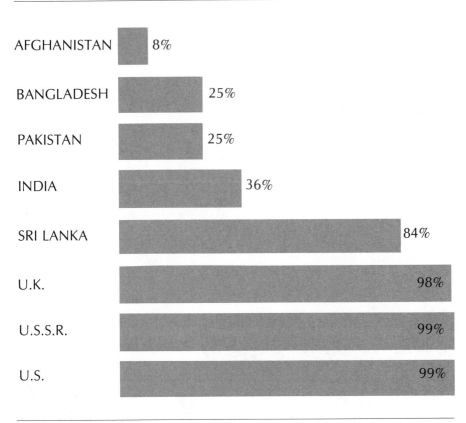

Source: *The 1980 World Almanac*

Use the bar graph above and information in Chapter 3 to answer the following questions.

1. What do the bars represent?

2. What is the source of the information in the graph?

3. Which country has the lowest proportion of people who can read or write?

4. In what country are about one in three people literate?

5. Why will Sri Lanka's literacy rate probably continue to be the highest of the subcontinent nations?

2
THE
CITY

Chapter 4

Where East Meets West

THE SUBCONTINENT'S LARGEST CITIES — Calcutta, Bombay, Delhi, Madras, and Hyderabad* in India, Karachi and Lahore in Pakistan, and Dacca* in Bangladesh — have two personalities.

One is modern. The cities have new office buildings and hotels. Wide boulevards carry more automobile traffic each year. Large apartment buildings and housing developments have shot up. Suburbs have spacious homes set in gardens ablaze with flowers. The cities and the suburbs also have large numbers of more modest houses for middle income families.

Department stores in the cities sell a wide variety of goods. In or near the cities of India and Pakistan are great industrial complexes. These textile mills, steel plants, and machinery factories employ thousands and use modern equipment. In Afghanistan, the only large city is Kabul. In Sri Lanka, Colombo is the only large city. There is less industrial development in these two countries than in India and Pakistan.

But the cities also have another personality. Forts,

palaces, temples, and shrines that are hundreds of years old lie scattered throughout many of them. New Delhi, India's capital, is built next to Delhi, which is a series of old cities. Delhi's ancient communities hold more than a thousand monuments of the past — some of them in near-perfect condition. These age-old buildings give the modern viewer some idea of the glory and magnificence of India's ancient civilizations.

For instance, in Delhi is a great palace inside a huge 300-year-old complex of buildings known as the Red Fort. A high, thick red sandstone wall with an intricate gateway surrounds the complex. One of these rooms has ceilings and walls of inlaid glass. Other walls were once studded with semiprecious stones. There were elaborate fountains, marble canals, and exquisite gardens. In the old days, dancing girls, perhaps as many as a hundred at a time, performed at night at the emperor's command. Musicians played, poets recited, and learned men told of ancient times and great battles.

Scented water ran in the baths. Delicious food odors hung lightly in the air. It must have been a scene of splendor that can scarcely be imagined today. On one of the walls was inscribed in the Persian language in golden letters:

> *If there is a paradise on earth,*
> *It is here! It is here! It is here!*

The subcontinent's most famous monument is the Taj Mahal* in the city of Agra. The Taj was built more than 300 years ago by an emperor as a tomb for his wife. (*Taj Mahal*, named in her memory, means "distinguished one of the palace.") Made of white marble by an army of laborers at a staggering cost, the Taj Mahal is one of the world's most beautiful buildings. As seen by moonlight, its perfect propor-

*Delhi's beautiful Red Fort, where princes studded
walls with semiprecious gems and inlaid glass.*

tions reflected in the long pool of water before it, the
Taj Mahal is a shimmering vision that casts a magic
spell (see page 116).

The town of Anuradhapura* in Sri Lanka was once
the capital of a great empire. Dozens of huge buildings and stone carvings completed as many as 2,000
years ago are reminders of its shadowy past. This
city was once famous throughout the ancient world
for the beauty of its buildings and the splendor of its
art.

It is not only through monuments by which the old
world lives on in the subcontinent. The full flavor of
this old world can best be experienced by a walk
through one of the *bazaar* (shopping) areas in the old
part of any large city. In Delhi, Chandni Chowk* —
"the square of moonlight" — is the main street of the

It is said that if people look long enough they can find anything they want in the bazaar.

biggest bazaar. Once it was a wide avenue down which emperors and princes rode on elephants with jeweled trappings. Now it is a crowded jumble of stores, people, and vehicles.

Many small streets lead from Chandni Chowk. Lanes and alleys branch from these side streets, and passageways seemingly without end stem from the alleys. As visitors walk deeper into the winding, narrow, crowded streets of the bazaar, they may feel that they can never find their way out.

Three- and four-story buildings line the streets of the bazaar. The upper floors are divided into small apartments which house big families. Shops occupy the ground floors. Most of the shops are very small, perhaps 10 to 12 feet wide and only a little deeper. Some may even be just four or five feet wide and a few feet deep.

The shop's owner sits cross-legged on a waist-high shelf. His stock of goods — combs, sunglasses, ballpoint pens — is piled up next to him. In a larger store, the owner often sits cross-legged on a wooden floor or on a raised platform covered with a white cotton cloth. Customers may sit on the platform with him and drink a cup of tea or coffee while making a purchase.

It is said that if people look long enough, they can find anything they want in the bazaar. There are ivory markets with carved figures of animals and Hindu gods and goddesses; brass markets; gem shops with sapphires, garnets, topazes, and moonstones; bamboo

shops; trinket shops with thousands of inexpensive arm and leg bracelets; book stalls; miniature foundries where men sweat over tiny blast furnaces as they handle red-hot pieces of metal; and bicycle repair sheds — all stretching out for block after block in noisy, colorful confusion.

One street is entirely filled with the shops of silversmiths. Another street has shops with beautiful carpets. Other shops are filled with great bolts of red, purple, gold, and green cottons and silks. Next to a cloth store is a tailor's shop where three men sit on straw mats. They are bent over their hand-powered sewing machines, carefully tailoring cloth into clothing. Another tailor is measuring a customer for a suit.

The art of bargaining reaches its height in the bazaar. When expert bargainers, who love a contest, confront each other, the purchase of an article is a long and delicate matter. The buyer doesn't simply ask the price and pay the first such price named. It is accepted that this figure is inflated and is merely the opening round. When the customer hears the first price, he offers half. The shopkeeper looks pained. He protests that his original price was already low, a special concession to the customer. Then the merchant quotes a figure somewhat lower than his first one.

Now it is the customer's turn to look pained. He claims that he can get the same article in a nearby store for much less — and he offers a bit more than he did before. After some minutes, perhaps including an interval when the customer indicates he is ready to walk out, a price will be agreed upon. The more expensive the item, the more subtle and prolonged the bargaining process. But not to bargain would be to miss half the challenge.

In the bazaar are tiny food counters with steaming

Sidewalk barber, squatting on ground as he plies his trade, is common sight in subcontinent's cities.

pots of potatoes, rice, and beans cooking over charcoal fires. In butcher shops, men are slicing meat with knives held between their toes. Fruit stalls are piled high with apples, oranges, raisins, bananas. Candy stands have syrupy sugar balls that dissolve in the mouth, and candies made with milk, sugar, and nuts. Some are covered with real silver so fine that it can be eaten.

In one place, a barber is squatting on the sidewalk, his tools spread out before him on a small cloth. Sitting opposite him is a customer, whom he is carefully shaving with a curved razor that looks like a small sickle. When he completes the shave, the barber cuts the customer's fingernails and toenails. Then the barber rubs oil vigorously into his customer's hair and over the bared upper half of his body.

All the while, the barber continues to squat. This is a position most westerners find hard to endure for more than a few minutes. The people of the subcontinent, however, can squat for an hour or more and not feel any strain. Many say they find it more comfortable to squat than to sit.

In a nearby lane, shoemakers are at work on the sidewalk. At the corner, a man squats before a stock of peanuts heated by a fire in a small pot. He sells the peanuts in tiny bags, or small pouches made of leaves pinned together, for about a penny a bag.

Next to the peanut seller is an old woman who looks 70, though she could just as well be less than 50. Her face is wrinkled, her hair white, her teeth missing, her feet bare, her ankles and wrists covered with bracelets, her body wrapped in a long piece of faded cloth. She is sitting before a pile of green bananas for sale. Beside her a naked child, perhaps her grandson, lies asleep.

Crowds are everywhere. The streets are noisy with children playing tag, jumping rope, spinning tops. Women are washing clothes in front of water pumps. Usually they scrub each piece and then pound it on a broad flat stone to beat out all the dirt. There are few washing machines in the subcontinent.

Trying to make their way through the bazaar are moving vehicles of every kind. It is said that Chandni Chowk is the site of the world's most tangled traffic jam. The streets are choked with cars, busses, taxis, scooters, bicycles, three-wheeled scooters with seats, horse-drawn carriages, buffalo-drawn carts, wandering animals. Sometimes a cow will lie down in the middle of a narrow street. No one forces the cow to move; rather the traffic must squeeze itself around the cow. Sometimes people on the sidewalks must also give way to cows which are considered sacred.

The cities of the subcontinent, especially in their bazaars, are alive and noisy, full of movement and tumult. And, despite their crowded quarters, stenches, and lack of job opportunities, they are getting larger each day as more and more people come into the cities from the villages.

More About India

A force of mounted sepoys (Indian soldiers) overrun a British supply train during the Indian mutiny of 1858.

THE END OF THE COMPANY

THE POWER OF THE British East India Company continued to expand through the first half of the 1800's.

Sometimes it took control by military force, sometimes by bribing high Indian officials. When it took over a state, the company either installed its own British governor or ruled through an Indian prince who was the company's puppet. The prince was constantly "advised" by a British official called the *resident*.

During those years the East India Company, besides using India as a source of raw materials and a market for goods manufactured in Britain, did much good for India. It built railroads and telegraph lines, dug irrigation canals, and installed a postal service. Coal mining was encouraged. Tea plantations were put on a commercial basis. Jute (fiber used for burlap bags) manufacturing was launched. The company profited from all these activities, of course, but many Indians became wealthy as well. After a considerable period of British rule, Indian businessmen started cotton mills, which competed with the mills of Britain for the Indian cloth market.

At the same time, however, the company expansion sometimes proceeded without regard for the feelings of the people. As we see throughout this book, Indian life was, and is, rooted in tradition and religion; and changes had to be made without offending traditional law and custom. The company administrators all too often did not choose to consider this fact. As a result, the British government had to take the subcontinent under its direct rule instead of governing it through the company. The East India Company was abolished and India was ruled by a system that derived its authority from the British Parliament.

The story of the company's end is this:

By the 1850's many Indian rulers were chafing under the expanding British power. They were angry at the way territories were annexed and rulers taken off their thrones. This anger filtered down to the company's Indian troops.

At that time most of the company's troops were Hindu or Moslem. About one in six or seven was British. Yet only the British could be commissioned officers; no Indian could reach a higher rank than that of petty officer. The Indians resented this discrimination, and they were angry at the company for sending them to fight in Burma, Persia, and China. They were also stirred up about a rumor that Hindus of different castes as well as Hindus and Moslems were to be forced to live and eat together. This was strictly contrary to their religious laws.

Thus furious, the Indian soldiers (called *sepoys**) needed only one more incident to revolt. The explosion came in 1857. The sepoys were instructed to bite off the greased tips of their new cartridges in order to pour the powder into their Enfield rifle muzzles. The word spread swiftly that the grease was a mixture of cow and pig fat.

The cow is sacred to the Hindu, and Moslems are forbidden to eat pork — so the order to bite off the cartridge tips was considered sinful in both religions. In vain the company protested that the grease was a vegetable fat. The revolt started at Meerut,* north of Delhi, and spread swiftly.

The Indian mutiny, or Sepoy Rebellion as historians now call it, raged for a year or more across northern India. Three great cities — Delhi, Kanpur, and Lucknow — were involved in the fighting. British employees of the East India Company and their families entrenched themselves in barricaded houses and estates and fought off the sepoy attacks. Many on both sides were slain. The rebellion was finally put down in 1858 by a combination of British troops and loyal sepoys.

England decided that the revolt was largely the fault of the East India Company — that it had administered India too long without considering the Indians themselves. Almost as soon as the Sepoy Rebellion was over, the British government took direct charge of India, with an appointed British official, called a *viceroy*, as head of state. India was, on the surface at least, more British than ever.

Double-check

Review

1. What city is India's capital?

2. What is the subcontinent's most famous monument?

3. What does the word *bazaar* mean in English?

4. Name two ways the East India Company used India.

5. Why did Indian soldiers refuse to bite off the tips of their cartridges?

Discussion

1. How is a subcontinent bazaar different from your community's main shopping area? How is it similar? Why do you think Indians bargain, but Americans generally don't? Which style of shopping would you prefer — bargaining, or paying whatever price is first stated? Why?

2. Despite the crowded conditions in the cities of the subcontinent, more people from the villages move in each day. Why do you think this is so? Could or should governments do anything to control this and other migrations of their citizens? If not, why not? If so, what could they do?

3. Do you think the East India Company was more interested in helping the Indians, or in helping themselves? Should a company that does business in a foreign country be forced to contribute to the welfare of the people in that country? Why, or why not?

Activities

1. Some students might draw or construct models of paintings, sculpture, crafts, or architecture of the ancient cities of the subcontinent as illustrated throughout this text.

2. Other students might research and report on the beauty of the Taj Mahal and Red Fort, preparing a bulletin board display of photographs and drawings.

3. Some students might role-play a bargaining session in an Indian bazaar.

Skills

STEPS TOWARD A MODERN SUBCONTINENT

3500 B.C.	**A.** Indian sepoys begin revolt.
1500–1200 B.C.	**B.** Vasco da Gama sails to Calicut.
326 B.C.	**C.** Indian mutiny put down.
Early 1400's	**D.** Dravidians invade subcontinent.
1498	**E.** Alexander the Great invades area.
c. 1500–1600	**F.** Robert Clive commits suicide.
1600	**G.** Aryans invade subcontinent.
1732	**H.** Indian constitution takes effect.
1757	**I.** Robert Clive victory at Plassey.
1774	**J.** East India Company chartered.
c. 1800–1850	**K.** Warren Hastings born.
1857	**L.** East India Company expands power.
1858	**M.** Portuguese control trade with India.
1950	**N.** Portuguese search for passage to India.

Chapters 1, 2, and 4 describe each of the events listed above. By using the timeline above and by going back through the chapters, do the following things on a separate sheet of paper.

1. List all the dates down the left side of your paper.

2. Using the information from the chapters, write the letter of each event next to the date on which it happened. (The events are *not* in the correct order in the above list.)

Chapter 5

Hari and Hemu

LIKE THE VILLAGES, the cities of the subcontinent are places of wretched poverty. In fact, the poverty of the cities often seems more grim than that of the villages because so many people are crowded so closely together.

Bombay, located on the shore of the Arabian Sea, is an Indian city of about six million people. One of the most modern cities on the subcontinent, it still contains numerous slums. Many of its poor live in shacks pieced together from tin, boards, bamboo grass, gunny sacking, and other scrap materials. The shacks were built as temporary shelters, but they became permanent dwelling places. There, children are born and raised, and families live in squalor and misery all their lives. Many such shacks are no more than 10 or 12 feet square and no higher than six or seven feet.

Even these people are not the worst off. Tens of thousands have no homes at all. They actually live in the streets, stretching out on the sidewalks or curling up in doorways at night to sleep.

One slum area of Bombay has at least 3,000 shacks, housing at least 13,000 people. The area has

Homeless and hopeless, an old man waits on a Calcutta street for someone to drop a coin that will help provide his next meal.

no more than 200 community water taps. And because of frequent water shortages, these taps sometimes give water for only a few hours a day. The community has no sanitation facilities at all. Piles of garbage are always present, as are insects and rodents. Vegetables and other foods sold in tiny stalls are sometimes completely covered with flies.

As in the villages, however, the people make great efforts to keep their homes clean. Most of them are washed down and swept twice a day. Almost everyone tries to bathe at least once a day, usually by pouring cupfuls of water over their bodies, then scrubbing themselves. There are no baths or showers and many people do not have soap to use.

Many of the children here never go to school, open a book, see a dentist, or have medical attention unless they are desperately sick. The boys will be looking for jobs by the time they are 12. Most of the girls will be married by 16 and grandmothers before they are 40.

The majority of men have unskilled jobs sweeping streets, carrying messages, pulling carts, working in factories. Some men are permanently unemployed. They want to work, but there are not enough jobs.

"He had left his family a long time ago," an Indian novelist wrote of a young man who had no home and slept on a bench in a corner of a big-city railroad station every night. "Three years was it? — as his brothers had done, as all the young men he knew had done or wanted to do, joining the exodus to the cities because their villages had nothing to offer them. The cities had nothing either, although they did not discover this until they arrived.

"If there had been a job, it might have been different, but there was no job. The colleges turned them out in the thousands each year — looking for employment, so what chance had he, with his meager elementary school learning?"

☆　☆　☆　☆　☆　☆　☆　☆　☆

Hari is 14 years old, slim, black-haired, handsome,

Despite poverty and lack of sewerage and running water, people try to keep themselves clean. This mother takes her baby to the well each day and pours a bucket of water over him.

intelligent. He lives with his parents and two sisters in a slum section of Delhi. Hari's home is 11 feet wide and 14 feet long, made of loosely joined bricks and tightly woven straw. It has an earth floor and no windows. The next house, which looks just like Hari's, is about four feet away.

Early every morning except Sundays and holidays, Hari walks about two miles to a busy Delhi corner. There he picks out a strategic spot on the sidewalk

73

and puts down his shoeshine box, squats behind it, and waits for customers. Next to him on the sidewalk, and at almost every other downtown corner, others are doing exactly the same. Some are boys of 10, and some are married men with families to support.

All day Hari squats behind his box. As people pass, he taps a shoe brush against the box to attract attention. He has no fixed price for a shine, but takes whatever a customer offers. Foreign visitors to the city sometimes give him as much as a rupee (13

Like thousands of other Calcutta families, this mother, her five children, and two pet dogs have no home. At night they sleep on the sidewalk.

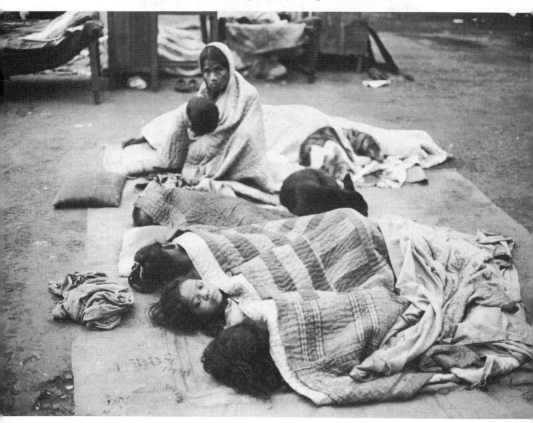

cents), but more often he receives about one quarter of a rupee. On good days, Hari makes as much as five rupees. Once or twice he has made double that.

Hari's average, however, is about two or three rupees a day. He gives his mother all the money he earns. She, in turn, gives him about two rupees a week for spending money. With this he usually buys sodas and cigarettes. Once, several years ago, he saved his allowance for a few weeks and went shopping with his friends. Then, as he recalls with great pleasure, they all went to a restaurant for a meal.

Hari never went to school. He can neither read nor write. He can speak a few words of English, picked up from tourists, in addition to his native language of Hindi. He does not think too much about his future, assuming he will go on doing more or less what he does now.

He sometimes talks about learning to read and write. Then he could go to a training school and be taught some skill such as operating a machine. His parents would like him to do this, but at the same time they need his earnings. Hari, in fact, is the family's steadiest wage earner.

Hari's father came to the city from a village in the western desert 20 years ago when he was 18. He hoped the city would offer him new opportunities. But since he was illiterate, he was forced to settle into a lifetime of low-paying jobs.

Hari's father works six and sometimes seven days a week, from just after dawn to just before dusk, at construction sites. He does a variety of jobs — mixes cement and sand to make concrete, assists the brick-layers, helps raise bamboo scaffolding, and unloads supplies from trucks. For this he receives four rupees a day. Usually there is plenty of work, but at times he is jobless for several weeks.

A luxury hotel under construction looms above a squalid Bombay slum. Rooms in the hotel will cost over $40 a day. The slum people consider themselves lucky to earn a few cents a day.

Hari's mother is a thin, short woman who looks much older than her 34 years. She also labors at construction sites, often alongside her husband. She works the same hours as he does but earns only three rupees a day. Much of the time she carries bricks to the bricklayers at work.

To do this she and her fellow brick bearers, all

**⊷§ The boys will be looking
for jobs by the time they are 12.
Most of the girls will be married
by 16 and grandmothers
before they are 40.**

women, place tightly wound coils of cloth on their heads. Then they put a flat board, two feet long and 10 inches wide, on the coil. On the board are placed 12 bricks, two at a time, working from the center outward so as to maintain the balance. When they have a full load they carry it to the bricklayers, sometimes several floors up. Somehow the women manage to walk with some grace even though the load is heavy. When there are no bricks to carry, Hari's mother sifts sand, digs trenches for pipes, or helps carry steel girders.

One of Hari's two sisters is a girl of 12. She works with her mother when the construction company needs more people. She too carries bricks and is just as skilled as her mother. She says she has never dropped a brick. The other sister, who is 10, stays at home and cares for the house or plays with friends. Neither of these girls has been to school, nor, as far as they know, has any of their girl friends.

As difficult as these conditions are, Hari's family is better off than some of its neighbors. One woman goes out each day with her nine-year-old daughter to beg. She sometimes takes along her youngest child, an infant of 18 months. She walks the streets for hours but does not manage to collect much more than a single rupee. Often she will walk alongside a foreigner for a block or more repeating "baksheesh, sahib" (money, sir) and gently touching his sleeve. Occasionally she will lay the baby down on the sidewalk directly in front of someone so that he must stop and, she hopes, give her some money.

Another woman goes to the railroad tracks. There she manages to fill a basket with pieces of half-burned coal. She sells the coal and uses the money to buy rice and vegetables. One man goes to business offices and asks for envelopes with used stamps. When he has collected enough stamps he puts them in a cardboard box and sells them. Another man stations himself near a tourist hotel and tries to sell his services as a guide.

Hemu is 57 years old and a lifelong resident of Calcutta, a city of eight million people. He is a human beast of burden. Working for a large transportation firm located in the dock area, he carries goods unloaded from ships to all parts of the city. He hauls these goods in a flat, two-wheeled cart. Often the load he pulls weighs 500 or more pounds, although Hemu himself weighs only 100 pounds. He tries to move at a trot because the momentum makes the going easier. But the load is often so heavy that this is impossible, and it even may take several men in the rear to push.

The work is hard at any time, but it is even harder during the summer when the heat is so intense that it softens the tar on the road. For his work Hemu receives an average of five rupees a day. Hemu considers himself fortunate that he has steady work. He is worried about what will happen in a few years when he will be too old to continue working. He has no savings and will receive no pension. He and his wife have no children to contribute to their support.

There are many millions like Hari and Hemu. There are many more millions even worse off with no jobs and no rupees coming in. Some live by begging and scavenging, others scrape by on odd jobs and gifts from relatives.

Double-check

Review

1. Why does the poverty of the cities often seem more grim than that of the villages?

2. The boys of Bombay will be looking for jobs by the time they are what age?

3. Why was Hari's father forced to settle into a lifetime of low-paying jobs?

4. How many people are even worse off than Hari and Hemu?

Discussion

1. What are your reactions to the photograph in this chapter of the family sleeping on the sidewalk? How are these people's lives different from the lives of the average family in your community? How do you account for the difference? Why do you think there is so much poverty in India? Why do you think there is poverty in the United States?

2. How are Hari's family responsibilities different from yours? How does your family depend on you? How do you depend on other members of your family? In your opinion, what would be the advantages and disadvantages of a 14-year-old playing such an important role in a family as Hari does?

3. To what extent should a society help its poor people? To what extent should the poor help themselves? In what ways does the U.S. government help the poor? Do you think there are different attitudes in the U.S. and in India toward the poor? Give reasons to support your answers.

Activities

1. A team of students might interview a representative of a local agency that helps poor people and then write an article about the agency's work for the school newspaper.

2. Some students might pretend to be Hari or Hemu meeting with representatives of the Indian government and telling them what kinds of programs they would like the government to establish in their communities.

3. A committee of students might prepare a report on Mother Teresa of Calcutta, a nun who won the 1979 Nobel Peace Prize for her work with the poor and sick of India.

Skills

Readers' Guide to Periodical Literature

March 1970 –February 1971

Page 594

INDIA—*Continued*

Nobility
Reprieve for the rajahs. il Time 96:21 D 28 '70

Parliament
Indira's big gamble: dissolution of Parliament. il Newsweek 77:49 Ja 11 '71

Politics and government
Eruption in India; tr. by J. Oringer. P. Gavi. il Ramp Mag 8:8+ Ap '70
Mrs. Gandhi's gamble. por Time 97:27–8 Ja 11 '71
World around us. V. Koilpillai. Chr Cent 87:974 Ag 12 '70
See also
Communist party (India)
India—Parliament
Political parties—India

Population
See also
Birth control—India

Relief work
Profiles; Missionaries of charity, Calcutta. V. Mehta. New Yorker 46:97–8+ Mr 21 '70

Abbreviations:

Ja — January

Mr — March

Ap — April

Ag — August

D — December

+ — continued on later pages

il — illustrated

tr — translated

por — portrait

Chr Cent — *Christian Century*

Ramp Mag — *Ramparts Magazine*

Use the above material from Readers' Guide to Periodical Literature *and information in Chapter 5 to answer the following questions.*

1. In which of the following publications will you find the articles listed in *Readers' Guide?*
(a) newspapers   (b) magazines   (c) books

2. How many articles on India are listed above?
(a) six   (b) three   (c) ten

3. How long a period of time is covered by this edition of *Readers' Guide?*
(a) two years   (b) two months   (c) one year

4. Under what letter of the alphabet would you look in *Readers' Guide* for listings of articles about Indian population control?
(a) B   (b) P   (c) C

5. In which magazines is there likely to be a story about people like Hari and Hemu?
(a) *Time*   (b) *Newsweek*   (c) *New Yorker*

Chapter 6

Other City People

HARI AND HEMU lead hard lives. Yet there are others for whom city life is easier or at least offers hope.

Joseph is 25 years old and the owner of a bicycle rickshaw in the large southern Indian city of Madras. Bicycle rickshaws are small, two-seat carriages linked to the front half of a bicycle. They serve as inexpensive taxis. Joseph has been pedaling such a rickshaw since he was 16. Saving his money, he managed to buy a rickshaw of his own several years ago. He hopes to have enough money soon to buy a second rickshaw and rent it out. Joseph has to work hard and his income is not large, but he is enthusiastic over the chance to earn more.

In the Bangladesh city of Dacca, a restaurant waiter says: "I work six days a week. My pay is about $23 a month, but I make about $15 more from tips. I try to live on as little as possible and send as much as I can to my wife and three children. They live in the village where I was born, about 50 miles from here. Right now I go home about once a month because the bus fare is costly. But I hope soon to have enough money to open a tea house in my own village."

Arvind, 48 years old, works in a large aluminum factory that employs more than 10,000 people in the southern part of India. He has been there for more than 25 years and today earns twice as much as he did 10 years ago. His salary is now about $5 a day. On this he supports a wife and three children. His home is a spotless two-room whitewashed cottage. In his small garden he grows tomatoes, cucumbers, and other vegetables.

Arvind and his children can read and write, but his wife cannot. All of his children, now in high school, would like to go to college. One son wants to be a chemical engineer, another a surgeon; his daughter wants to be a children's doctor. Even though it will be a hard financial burden, Arvind is determined that each will have the chance to go to college.

Zakir is a 28-year-old welder in a shipyard which uses the most modern equipment and methods. He works on the construction of steel fishing boats. His pay, including all fringe benefits, comes to more than $6 a day. This means that he is among the most highly paid industrial workers in the subcontinent. He hopes to gain a foreman's position soon.

Zakir, his wife, and three children live in a three-room apartment in a 50-year-old building. By the standards of the subcontinent, the apartment is well furnished. In addition to beds, a table and chairs, dressers, and a couch, the apartment has a refrigerator, a sewing machine, a phonograph, and a radio.

Usha is 18 years old and lives with her parents and sister in a comfortable home in a city of about 150,-000 people. A first-year student in an institute of

*The cities of the Indian subcontinent contain
people of all income levels and education.
Above: a busy Bombay street corner.*

> ◈ **"I am the first girl in my family ever to have gone to a university. When I first told my father my plans he was so astonished he didn't know what to say."**

technology, she is taking a five-year engineering course. When she is graduated, she wants to continue her studies abroad, then return to India to work.

"I am the first girl in my family ever to have gone to a university," Usha says. "When I first told my father my plans he was so astonished he didn't know what to say. He wasn't surprised that I wanted to go to a university, just that I wanted to be an engineer. Some of my relatives thought there must be something wrong with a girl who wished such things. They didn't think it proper for a girl to study engineering. But I insisted, and everyone finally agreed."

Usha's sister is in the sixth grade. She attends a large modern school which has about 500 students. She studies Punjabi, the local language; Indian history; mathematics; and Indian literature. She also studies English and, like her sister, speaks it well.

Usha's father is a government official who has been working in the Department of Agriculture for 15 years. His pay is 1,800 rupees a month. This makes him one of the more highly paid government officials in the country. When he retires he will have a comfortable pension. He has degrees from three universities and has been to the United States and Europe on government missions. He speaks perfect English, in addition to Punjabi, Marathi, and several other

*This Indian girl, from a wealthier family,
is a student at an agricultural college.*

Indian languages. His wife, who does not work, is also
fluent in English.

Their home has two bedrooms, a living room, a
dining room, and a kitchen. It is comfortably furnished — including several beautiful rugs, a number

of wood carvings, and some art work in brass. The family owns a refrigerator, a hi-fi set, an expensive camera, and a car. Once a year the family takes a good vacation. Next year it is planning to go north to the resort area of Kashmir. There the family plans to rent a houseboat on one of the lakes.

Some live even more comfortably than Usha's family. These are generally businessmen, industrialists, and others whose income may be thousands of rupees a month. They usually have very large homes and three or four servants. One man has an income of 7,500 rupees ($975) a month. His wife has many servants. One does the cooking; a second serves the food; a third does the cleaning; a fourth is the gardener and handy man; a fifth is a part-time laundryman. The total salary of all five servants comes to $64 a month. Only a few families can afford to keep a number of servants.

The cities of the subcontinent contain people at all income levels. But the well-off or even moderately well-off are in the minority. The majority of the people are very poor. However, many cities have been enjoying great economic growth in recent years. This has brought new job opportunities and new hope to many.

Bal Gangadhar Tilak, left, and Gopal Krishna Gokhale, two of the earliest fighters for Indian independence from Britain.

MARCH TOWARD INDEPENDENCE

MANY INDIANS STILL THINK of the Sepoy Rebellion as India's first war for independence. Yet there were almost 90 years between 1858, the end of the revolt, and 1947, when independence was finally achieved. For most of those 90 years, the British were firmly in control of business and government. In 1877, for example, Britain's Queen Victoria was also crowned Empress of India in a dazzling coronation ceremony held in Delhi.

During the first years after the rebellion, the Indians were divided and leaderless. The few wealthy people at the top had no links with the hundreds of millions of poor and oppressed below them. Hindus continued their age-old quarrel with Moslems. Indians were barred from important posts in the government. True, there were Hindu maharajas and Moslem nawabs who ruled the hundreds of large and small "princely" (or "native") states. But they were only figurehead rulers, even though some were fabulously wealthy. The real voice of authority was British.

After 1858 the Indian army was shaken up from top to bottom. Only those sepoys who had remained loyal in the revolt were kept in the service. More British soldiers were brought in to replace the discharged Indians. Soon one in three was British, contrasted to the one in six or seven before the rebellion.

Another big change took place in the economy after the revolt. Indians had been making their own products, mainly by hand, from their own raw materials. Now the raw materials were shipped to Britain. There they were turned into cheap manufactured goods and sent back for sale in India.

Handmade Indian items could not be sold as cheaply as these factory-made British wares. As a result, Indians who had been making textiles, metal goods, even ships — all without the aid of heavy machinery — were thrown out of work. The telegraph lines and the railroads which were helping to industrialize India were shipped from Britain. Shipments of manufactured goods increased when the Suez Canal was opened in 1869. It cut transport time between London and Bombay from three months to less than one month.

For a long time after the Sepoy Rebellion, most of the British in India feared and distrusted the Indians. They could not forget the killings and atrocities that had taken place in 1857-58. In turn, the Indians grew even more hostile toward the British. Many liberal British leaders tried hard to make both Indians and Britons rid themselves of hate.

One such leader was Allan Octavian Hume, a retired British government official in India. In 1883 he sent a letter to the graduates of Calcutta University, telling them: "Whether in the individual or the nation, all vital progress must spring from within, and it is to you, its most cultured and enlightened minds, its most favored sons, that your country must look for the initiative." He was saying that the British would help, but that the Indians themselves must take the lead in improving their land and the lives of its people.

Hume's aim was to start an Anglo-Indian group that would work for the good of India. Instead, these university graduates began their own movement, and Hume worked with them. The movement became the Indian National Congress, the first political party in the country and today still among the strongest.

One leader of the new movement was Bal Gangadhar Tilak,* a Brahman and a revolutionary who advocated violent methods. He struck out for immediate independence. He announced, "*Swaraj**[freedom] is my birthright, and I will have it!" He did not live to see India reach freedom — but he helped start it on its way.

Another early leader of the Indian National Congress was Gopal Krishna Gokhale.* Like Tilak, he too wanted India free. Unlike Tilak, however, Gokhale was a moderate who emphasized getting along with the British. A practical man, he wanted freedom won without violence and disorder.

Gokhale died in 1915; Tilak in 1920. Midway between those years a new leader came forward, one who combined Tilak's zeal with Gokhale's practical sense. He was Mohandas K. Gandhi (see page 139), who planned and led India's march to independence.

A century ago, British colonial administrators traveled in style, if not comfort, when they toured countryside.

Double-check

Review

1. What are bicycle rickshaws?

2. What subjects does Usha's sister study?

3. What proportion of the people in subcontinent cities are very poor?

4. What do many Indians still think of as India's first war for independence?

5. When the Suez Canal was opened in 1869, how much did it cut transport time between London and Bombay?

Discussion

1. Does there seem to be a relationship between income and formal education in India? Is it usually true in the United States that the more education people have, the more money they make? Should this be true? Can you name examples where this might be true, and examples where it might not be true? How do you judge the value of education in terms of money? Explain your answers.

2. Do you think some careers or occupations — such as engineering — should be held only by men, and other careers or occupations should be held only by women? Give reasons to support your answer.

3. The British barred Indians from important posts in the government. Why do you think the British had this policy? Do you think the policy was fair? Why, or why not? Was it self-defeating?

Activities

1. Some students might research and report on the similarities between the colonial American and the colonial Indian struggle for national independence. Students could compare how Britain treated colonists in America and in India, and how the Americans and Indians reacted to this treatment.

2. Some students might write a diary from the point of view of Usha's sister as she contrasts her life with the lives of the poor people she sees each day. Include what feelings she might have about the differences between her life and the lives of the poor.

3. While role-playing, one student might pretend to be Bal Gangadhar Tilak or a follower, and another student could pretend to be Gopal Krishna Gokhale or a follower. The two could debate the topic "How To Free India from British Control."

Skills

MAP READING

Use the map on page 13 and information in Chapter 6 to answer the following questions. On a separate sheet of paper, write the number of each question. Then write the letter or letters of the best answer or answers next to the number of each question.

Answers

(A) **Brazil**

(B) **India**

(C) **Population**

(D) **Sri Lanka**

(E) **Per Capita Income**

(F) **Afghanistan**

(G) **Less**

(H) **Kenya**

(I) **More**

1. What does the bottom number in each box represent?

2. In which country do most people on the Indian subcontinent live?

3. Which subcontinent country has the smallest increase in population every year?

4. Outside the Indian subcontinent, which country has the lowest per capita income level?

5. Does the waiter in the Bangladesh city of Dacca earn more or less than the average person in his country?

THE LAND

Immense and changing, the subcontinent's terrain sweeps from
cities such as Varanasi on Ganges
(below), to snow-covered mountains on Nepalese border (right),
or to one of hundreds of thousands
of villages (lower right), with their
thatch-roofed mud huts.

WATER: Much of the subcontinent is arid, watered only by streams (above), by man-made irrigation channels (below), or by fitfully flowing wells (right). None of these produces a dependable supply.

ANIMALS: Elephants that haul logs (below), sheep that give wool (right), live close to people in India, but it is the cow which is closest. Cows are considered sacred and are never killed. Cow wanders unnoticed through Delhi streets (below right).

POVERTY: The subcontinent is poor — and shows it in many ways: the New Delhi slum (above), the Bengali market (below), and the Bombay street (right), with its vehicles pulled by animals or human beings.

THE PEOPLE

The population of the subcontinent
is quite diverse. Some are very rich;
some middle class. But vast majority
are pathetically poor. Pomp of
preindependence maharajah (above)
and plight of a hungry child (right)
tell story of few rich, many poor.

CONTRASTS: Sikh
farmers (far left) are
part of small middle
class. Well-to-do
(lower left), an even
smaller class, watch
golf match. Country
and city poor (left and
below) live under
conditions that most
Americans would find
unbelievably wretched.

NORTHERN INDIANS: In northern India, which borders on Tibet, Nepal, and Bhutan, the native people look more Mongolian than Indian. In recent years there has been increasing unrest in these areas and hostility toward the central government.

TASKS: Endless toil is way of life on the subcontinent. Sri Lankan craftsmen (above) make pottery. Pakistani woman (below) cooks. Young boys (right) carry firewood. Madras driver (far right) rests oxen before loading his cart with freight.

THE ECONOMY

Despite expanding industries and productive mines, the subcontinent's economy is mainly agricultural, as indicated by scenes of winnowing grain (left), vegetable market (top), and planting rice.

109

MUSCLE POWER: The economy of the subcontinent is rapidly expanding, but the primary source of power remains the human body. Laborers carry coal to a pumping station (upper left). Longshoremen unload rice from freighter's hold (lower left). Laborer pulls cartload of fibers (above). Villagers haul in catch on beach in Sri Lanka (below).

PROGRESS: Poor, ignorant, tradition-shackled —
yet the subcontinent moves forward, as demonstrated
by Pakistani gas field (upper left), Pakistani institute
of chemical technology (left), Indian steel mill
(above), Indian villagers building road (below).

113

SKILLFUL HANDS: Many people of
the subcontinent are skilled in crafts
as shown by woman adjusting gauges
(above), craftsman embroidering silk
sheet with gold thread (below), men
blocking designs on fabric (right).

THE CULTURE

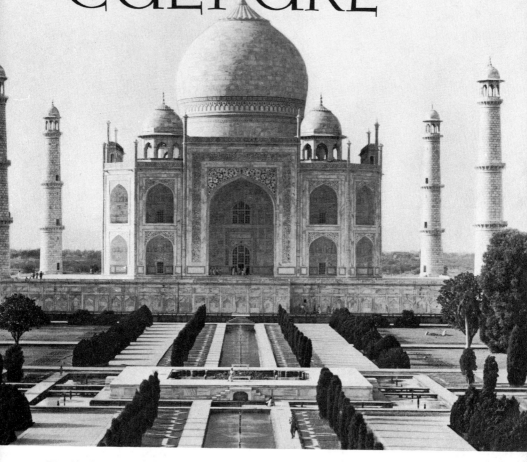

Religion—mainly Hinduism, Islam, Buddhism—dominates the culture of the subcontinent. Above, the classically beautiful Moslem tomb called the Taj Mahal, built by a Moslem emperor for his wife in the 17th century. Right, a statue of the Hindu deity Siva, pictured with several arms, symbolizing his several different powers.

HINDU, MOSLEM, AND BUDDHIST:
Each has own rites and beliefs.
Moslem faithful pray at the end of holy
month of Ramadan (below). Buddhist
monks in Sri Lanka gather under gaze of
Buddha (above right). A Hindu swami
(holy man) performs rituals at
a funeral ceremony (right).

GALA: *Musicians play for dancers (upper left). Boys dance on stilts (lower left). Sikh priests read marriage rites (above). Cobras perform for "charmers" (below).*

EDUCATION: Schools on the subcontinent vary widely in quality. In New Delhi science class (above), teacher demonstrates method. Elementary school in poor farm village meets outdoors (below). Sometimes (right), the "school" is a field and there are no desks or chairs and only one or two books.

3
CASTE
AND
FAMILY

NOTICE

THIS WELL IS OPEN TO ALL CLASSES
INCLUDING SCHEDULED CASTES.

نوٹس

اِس کوئیں سے ہر جماعت کے لوگ جنہیں ہریجن بھی
شامل ہیں پانی لے سکتے ہیں

Chapter 7

Caste: A Way of Living

GOVINDAN, AGE 22, had just returned to his south Indian village from the university where he had completed his law studies. He was walking with his father, who owned a small paint factory, along a village street. Govindan stopped at a well set in a little square. It was hot; Govindan was thirsty. He began to lower the bucket to get a drink.

For a moment his father stood silent. Then, angry, he ordered Govindan away from the well. The reason for his anger was that this well was for a certain *caste* (social group) in the village — and for that caste only. This was a lower caste than the one to which Govindan belonged. So he would have defiled himself, and his family as well, by drinking water from the well. The possibility of defilement was what had upset Govindan's father.

Govindan, like millions of others in India, no longer believed in caste customs, but he was not

125

ready to defy them. Thus he obeyed his father immediately. Not to have done so, to have drunk the well water, would have been a serious violation of custom in the village, which still followed the traditional ways.

Indeed, if Govindan had remembered to which caste the well belonged, he never would have come near it. Although caste customs are becoming weaker each year in India, they are still powerful in many places, particularly the villages. In fact, caste customs are responsible for much of the condition of Indian society today.

Long centuries ago the Indian people began to divide into different groups, or classes. At first these were only separate classes, without the caste codes which arose later. Then the most powerful groups found a way to strengthen and preserve their own privileges and position. At the top was a group called Brahmans. These were the priests and teachers. Next to the Brahmans were the statesmen and soldiers. Merchants and farmers made up the third. Common laborers and workers (serfs) were in the fourth and lowest group.

The first three groups are known even today as the *twice born*. Boys in these castes pass through a special ceremony when they are 10. A priest anoints the boy with oil, chants sacred verses, then ties a sacred thread around the boy's body. He is now considered to have been born again. The thread, a reminder of caste obligations, will be worn until it rots away. Then it will be replaced many times during the boy's life.

Each of the four groups once had a carefully worked-out set of obligations and rights. The duty of the merchant and farmer caste, for instance, was to engage in commerce and trade and increase the

126

wealth of the land. The ancient codes instructed a member of this group to know "the prices of mercantile commodities, especially of gems, pearls, coral, iron, cloth, perfumes, and liquids. He must be skilled in sowing seeds, in the qualities of land, in weights and measures, in the excellence and defects of articles of traffic, in the advantages and disadvantages of different districts, in the probable gain and loss on goods, in the breeding of cattle, in the wages of servants, in the various languages of men, in the best place for keeping cattle...."

By about the third century B.C., when the caste system began to take over the old four-class society, laws spelled out the relations between the castes. In later centuries these laws became a complex code. A Hindu could not marry someone of another caste. Nor could Hindus eat with those of a lower caste. It was equally forbidden for them to eat with people of a higher caste. Social functions such as weddings could not be attended by people of different castes.

Seating was another important aspect of caste. One student of Indian customs wrote: "The height of a seat one occupies is in direct ratio to the social position of the occupant. A man of lower caste cannot sit in the presence of a man of higher caste. Men of the same caste, but having different social positions on account of differences in wealth or on account of some prejudice, may sit in one another's presence, but the lesser man must be careful to occupy a lower seat than his superior. If seats of the correct height are not available, the lesser man must stand. Social position being equal, age decides seniority."

Many of the ancient rules made clear the relative positions of the castes down to the most trivial detail. For instance, the stick which a Brahman used to brush his teeth had to be 12 inches long. A man from

> **If a low-caste person were ...to attack a Brahman, the person would be sentenced to death. But if a Brahman [attacked a low caste], the Brahman would only be reprimanded for becoming polluted....**

the warrior caste was instructed to use a stick 11 inches long. The two lower castes were told to use sticks of 10 and nine inches.

Those in the higher castes, particularly the Brahmans, enjoyed many privileges under the old social system. If a low-caste person were for some reason to attack a Brahman, the person would be sentenced to death. But if a Brahman were to attack a low-caste person, the Brahman would only be reprimanded for becoming polluted by touching an inferior being.

It was the duty of all other castes to support the Brahmans, to give them money, food, and shelter if needed. If a man gave a Brahman a house, some of the codes said, the donor would be blessed with a palace in heaven. If he gave a Brahman a red cow, he would after death receive safe and swift passage across a terrifying river that the dead encountered on the way to the next world.

Brahmans, in turn, were instructed to be thrifty, kind, satisfied, and generous. They were never to get angry or tell lies, never to sing or dance, never to use an umbrella or wear sandals because this would make them too comfortable, and never to eat any kind of meat or kill any living thing.

Over the centuries, the four major castes were divided into thousands of subcastes. These subcastes were then divided into clans. The exact subcaste and clan to which a family belonged determined the specific occupation of the men in the family and the exact god or goddess which the family worshipped.

For example, two men who belonged to the fourth caste, that of the laborers and workers, were in separate subcastes if the work they did differed. A carpenter and a blacksmith would not be in the same subcaste. Two men in the same subcaste might be in different clans if their families worshipped different gods. To complicate matters further, in some cases two families in different subcastes might regard themselves as particularly close if they happened to worship the same god.

Just as each of the major castes had regulations governing behavior, so each of the subcastes had its own exact rules. These covered every phase of life. For instance, the value and kind of gift one subcaste member should give to a member of another subcaste at various ceremonies was often specified. To give too much or too little was equally bad and could upset village relationships.

Within the subcaste system, some groups enjoyed a higher status than others. Just as a Brahman could not meet a member of a worker caste socially, so a member of a worker caste would not want to socialize with another worker of a lower subcaste.

The result of all this was an incredibly complex social system governed by an elaborate set of rules. It was an absolutely rigid system because people could not change the subcaste into which they had been born.

Outside the caste system entirely was still another group — the Untouchables. These were people whose work was sweeping streets, picking up refuse, treating animal hides, disposing of dead animals. Such work was thought to make them unclean.

By custom in some parts of India, when a Brahman dies, his relatives search out an Untouchable and give him a gift. Here eldest son performs the custom, making sure he does not pollute himself by touching the Untouchable.

Strict rules governed the behavior of the Untouchables and their relations with other groups. According to these rules, most of which are no longer strictly observed, Untouchables were not to come into any contact with caste members. Their touch or shadow was considered to be defiling or polluting.

In some regions, Untouchables had to wear tinkling bells around their necks to warn people of their coming. Before entering the gates of one city, Untouchables had to ring a gong hung at the entrance and so signal their approach.

If an Untouchable were fixing a fence in a narrow lane, he had to post signs of his presence at both entrances to the lane. Sweepers in some cities could not appear outside their homes without a broom. The broom immediately told who they were. Untouchables could be admitted to the courtyard of a high caste family. But they could under no circumstances step on the veranda. This would put them on an equal footing with a caste member.

Similarly, Untouchables had to step aside as caste members passed. Everything was so arranged that an Untouchable would always be in an inferior position, always reminded of his or her status.

Certain Untouchables were also "unlookables." It was forbidden for them to show their faces in daylight or for Brahmans to look upon them. In some parts of India, Untouchables might be punished if their shadows fell across the body of a Brahman. In order to lessen the chance of such an occurrence, several cities passed strict laws that forbade all Untouchables to enter the central part of town after the middle of the afternoon. By that time their shadows were long and in danger of falling on a Brahman.

To make sure that Untouchables did not forget their lowly status, they were forbidden to build houses of stone or wood. They had to limit their dwellings to mud and straw. They were not allowed to own land, wear good clothes, or even try to obtain the kinds of work considered clean.

The complex set of rules governing Untouchables and castes developed over the centuries. Thus Indian society became divided into thousands of water-tight compartments, each containing one subcaste or group having little contact with the rest of society. Within a compartment all people were equal, but there was little equality in the society at large.

Double-check

Review

1. Why was Govindan's father angry with him?

2. What is responsible for much of the condition of Indian society today?

3. What would happen if a low-caste person were to attack a Brahman?

4. What duty did all other castes have toward Brahmans?

5. What determined the specific occupation of the men in the family and the exact god or goddess which the family worshipped?

Discussion

1. How much might the caste system have to do with the condition of poverty-stricken people in India? Why? What effect might prejudice or discrimination have on the motivation or ability of people to succeed — in any society?

2. What are "rites of passage"? Could the ceremony for some 10-year-old Indian boys be called a rite of passage? What are some examples of rites of passage — formal or informal — that young people in the U.S. experience as they become adults? What are the values of such ceremonial markings of life's stages? What importance do they have to society? What importance do they have to the young person involved in them?

3. What kinds of discrimination are found in American society? Do you think this discrimination is as harsh as it is in India? Is it possible to escape being the victim of discrimination in the U.S.? Give examples to support your answer.

Activities

1. In a role-playing activity, two students might recreate the scene at the beginning of the chapter. But this time, the student playing Govindan could protest the caste custom concerning the well, and try to convince his father that it was all right for him to drink from the well. The "father" (or, if the student is female, "mother") could disagree and try to explain why customs are still important to village society.

2. Some students might draw political cartoons or posters depicting an aspect of prejudice or discrimination in India or the U.S. Afterward, the class could hold a contest to choose the best poster.

3. Some students might research and report on religious rites of passage in several different societies.

Skills

USING AN INDEX

Use the above listings from the Index to this book and information in Chapter 7 to answer the following questions.

1. In what order are topics listed in an index?
(a) by importance   (b) by page numbers   (c) alphabetically

2. What do the numbers after each topic stand for?
(a) ages   (b) chapter references   (c) page references

3. On what page would you find an illustration of Chandni Chowk?
(a) 59   (b) 62   (c) 61

4. On how many pages in this text is the caste system dealt with?
(a) eight   (b) 16   (c) 18

5. About when would the item that has the greatest number of entries in this Index not have rated such a large entry in a book on India?
(a) before the third century B.C.   (b) before 1945   (c) before 1600

Chapter 8

Caste Today

THE STRENGTH OF THE CASTE SYSTEM and the prejudice against Untouchables have both been declin-
ing steadily since the start of the 1900's. It is now
forbidden by law to discriminate against an Untouchable. Children of Untouchables now sit next to Brahman children in school. Caste Hindus have married
Untouchables. There are many poor Brahmans and
some wealthy Untouchables.

The growth of democratic ideas and the lifelong
efforts of such men as Gandhi and Nehru (*see* pages
139 and 182) have led to the gradual weakening of
caste and untouchability. Many Indians regard these
as systems which may once have helped society maintain some order. Now, however, they are regarded as
outdated and evil. The old caste system might have
worked in a rural setting. But most observers believe
that it is out of place in a society striving to industrialize. For caste hampers people's freedom and mo-
bility, so necessary for industrial growth.

Nevertheless, ideas which were believed for centu-

An Untouchable family in a section of the slums of Bombay occupied only by Untouchables. Although discrimination against Untouchables is lessening, it is still a serious problem for India.

ries and which were so important do not die easily. In the villages many caste customs and restrictions, even if not as faithfully observed as before, are still practiced. For instance, the homes of the members of each caste are usually found together in one section. A low caste member or an Untouchable would not think of moving to the Brahman area of the village, nor would Brahmans move out of their own quarter. The well in each area used to be for the exclusive use of that caste. In practice this remains generally true, although signs may proclaim that anyone may use the well.

Members of upper castes usually bathe thoroughly at the day's end, not only to remove dirt but sometimes to remove "pollution" picked up from contact with lower castes. In the cities, however, crowded conditions and other aspects of urban life have reduced the strength of caste customs.

In some villages each caste has its separate council house, with another council house for affairs which concern the entire village. Strangers are always welcome at the council houses of their castes. But they are not normally allowed to enter the council house of a higher caste, nor would they attempt to do so.

In the other countries of the subcontinent, a caste system as strict as that in most of Hindu India never developed. Instead, an equally complicated system of relationships based on jobs formed the basis of village society. In Hindu India the caste into which a boy was born decided his future occupation. In Moslem Pakistan, Afghanistan, and Bangladesh, and Buddhist Sri Lanka, trades were handed down from father to son. The result was similar across the subcontinent.

In each village there were families who were always the barbers, carpenters, pottery makers, blacksmiths, tailors, and other nonfarmers. Each of these

Damodaram Sanjivayya, an Untouchable who rose to be chief minister of Andhra Pradesh state in India.

workers supplied their goods or services to a number of families. These relationships lasted for generations. In return, the families served gave the workers money, grain, clothing, and other needed items. On holidays and special occasions, both families and workers might receive something extra. This system of mutual service was widespread.

In this way, all the workers in the village knew exactly what their obligations were — and to whom — and more or less what they could earn. In the insecure world of the subcontinent, this system offered great security. By giving everyone an exact place in the village scheme of things, the system did away with competition. Since workers did not have to compete, they could cooperate.

The system put heavy pressure upon any young man who refused to follow the family vocation. If the son persisted in wanting to be a blacksmith when his family occupation was carpentry, he might even have to leave the village. He was a threat to established relationships.

Moslem and Buddhist men were not free to choose their occupations any more than Hindus were free to choose their caste. This was not a matter of tyranny, but of survival. Suppose those who were expected to follow the carpenter's trade refused to do so. Then how would farm implements be fixed? Even if just one man refused to follow the hereditary occupation, the entire structure of the village economy could be endangered.

A village might find itself without some essential worker, perhaps because the man in that occupation had no sons. Then it would send a delegation to other villages in the district to recruit someone who could be spared. For example, a blacksmith in another village might have two sons, but his village had enough work for only one. Then the second son could be invited to go to another village. Perhaps that other village might try to make the offer more attractive. It could promise the man a house or, if he were unmarried, a bride.

Whatever the problem, there was an old rule to solve it. But in time these rules impeded progress, because they gave only old answers to new difficulties.

Mohandas Karamchand Gandhi

GANDHI: GREAT SOUL

HE WAS A LITTLE MAN, bald and almost toothless. His steel-rimmed spectacles perched precariously half-way down his nose. He customarily wore a *dhoti,** a sheetlike garment wrapped around the waist, and sandals. His voice was soft, almost weak, and his smile was gentle and disarming.

Despite his birth in a prominent family and his British university education, he was in tune with the villagers of the subcontinent. This man — humble in manner, modest in appearance — led India to unity and independence. It was a true revolution against Britain, but it was won by nonviolent means. And nonviolence was the key to this man's leadership. His people called him "Mahatma" (Great Soul). His real name was Mohandas Karamchand Gandhi.

Gandhi was born October 2, 1869, in Porbandar, India. His father was the prime minister of the little state of Porbandar. His mother was a devout Hindu, always ready to give much of herself to others. The family was of the merchant caste (see page 126), but young Mohandas chose an Untouchable as his best friend. Early in life he was rebelling against the system that kept India divided and backward.

His parents arranged a marriage (see page 157) for Mohandas when he was 13. His bride was Kasturba, whose family was also of the merchant caste. After the wedding, young Gandhi continued going to school. In his late teens he decided to study law at the University College in London. Against the wishes of his family, he sailed for England alone. During his first months in London he tried to turn himself into an English gentleman. He soon gave up the impossible task and settled down to the serious study of law. At the same time he read many books that talked about changing society.

Back home in India, Gandhi opened a law office, but few clients knocked on his door. In 1893 an Indian who had settled in South Africa asked him to do some legal work. Gandhi went to South Africa, intending to stay only several months. He remained for 21 years.

Many Indians had come to South Africa as laborers, and a number later became merchants. At that time South Africa was under Britain's control. The Indians suffered severe discrimination. Gandhi became the leading lawyer for these people. He fought for their rights in the courts and in the legislature.

The British authorities arrested him many times, but he fought on. Always his resistance was passive, his battles nonviolent. By the time he returned to India, his countrymen in South Africa had been granted greater respect and fairer treatment by the government.

In India once more, Gandhi found himself a hero because of his South African accomplishments. He set about learning India's problems anew, riding in the third-class sections of trains or walking from village to village. Soon he became leader of the Indian National Congress. He constantly preached nonviolence, and when his followers rioted he fasted until they promised to stop.

One demonstration of his leadership was in the Amritsar* Massacre of 1919. A large but peaceful crowd had assembled to protest a ban on Gandhi's visit to the town of Amritsar. Seeing the huge numbers of people, the British general ordered his troops to fire into the crowd. Nearly 400 were slain. Only Gandhi's influence prevented a mass uprising as a result of the shooting.

Gandhi was nonviolent, but he was extremely active. For example, he launched a campaign to teach the villagers how to spin cotton by hand. He wanted Indians to stop depending on the British for cloth — and for many other things — and to begin getting along by themselves.

But the British continued to pass laws that blocked Indian freedoms. One law made it illegal to possess salt on which a tax had not been paid to the government. Accompanied by hundreds of his followers, Gandhi made a 200-mile march to the sea. There he extracted salt from the sea water. For this Gandhi was jailed, as he had been many times before. In prison he read, wrote, fasted, and prayed. In time the authorities had to release him. He spent a total of seven years in prison for such offenses, but he continued to risk arrest for the sake of India's cause.

Gandhi rejoiced when independence was won in 1947 (see page 162). But he grieved to see the partition of the subcontinent into a Hindu India and Moslem Pakistan. He had always preached that Hindus and Moslems should live in peace. He was murdered in 1948 as he prepared to attend a prayer meeting. His killer, another Hindu, hated Gandhi for trying to bring members of the two religions together.

Double-check

Review

1. What has led to the gradual weakening of caste and untouchability?

2. What would a village do if it found itself without some essential worker?

3. What was the key to Gandhi's leadership?

4. When Gandhi's followers rioted, what did he do?

5. Who murdered Gandhi, and why did he do it?

Discussion

1. In what ways do the caste system and the system of inherited occupations produce social stability? Why is stability important to a society? Is stability more important to a society than individual freedom? Why, or why not?

2. Why do democratic ideas often appear when a society decides to industrialize? Why is the spirit of competition important to an industrialized society? How could cooperation between workers and the system of inherited occupations hinder a society's efforts to industrialize? Would you prefer to work in a society that emphasizes cooperation or one that emphasizes competition? Why?

3. Do you think Gandhi would have been as effective as he was if he had advocated violence? Explain your answer.

Activities

1. Jagjivan Ram, an Untouchable, was an unsuccessful candidate in the 1980 election for the prime minister of India. If Ram had been elected, he would have been the first Untouchable to be prime minister. Some students might write campaign speeches for Ram to deliver to a large crowd of wealthy Indians. They could take turns delivering their speeches to the class.

2. A member of a group that advocates nonviolent methods of achieving change might be invited to speak to the class on the aims of the group and how it tries to achieve these aims through nonviolence.

3. Some students might research and report on the life and thoughts of Gandhi, being sure to investigate the influence of Thoreau on Gandhi's thoughts about nonviolence and society.

Skills

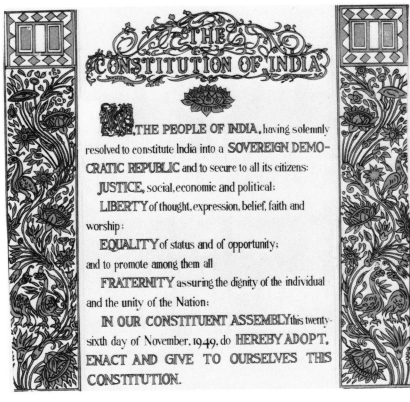

THE CONSTITUTION OF INDIA

WE, THE PEOPLE OF INDIA, having solemnly resolved to constitute India into a SOVEREIGN DEMOCRATIC REPUBLIC and to secure to all its citizens:

JUSTICE, social, economic and political;

LIBERTY of thought, expression, belief, faith and worship;

EQUALITY of status and of opportunity;

and to promote among them all

FRATERNITY assuring the dignity of the individual and the unity of the Nation;

IN OUR CONSTITUENT ASSEMBLY this twenty-sixth day of November, 1949, do HEREBY ADOPT, ENACT AND GIVE TO OURSELVES THIS CONSTITUTION.

Use the passage above and information in Chapter 8 to answer the following questions.

1. What part of the constitution is this?
(a) an amendment   (b) the body   (c) the preamble

2. Which Indian citizens are affected by this constitution?
(a) all   (b) the assembly   (c) sovereign democrats

3. Who "gave" this constitution to India?
(a) England   (b) the assembly   (c) the people of India

4. How many years after India won its independence was this constitution adopted?
(a) three years   (b) two years   (c) one year

5. Which of the following phrases probably best describes the situation between the castes in India today?
(a) justice without liberty   (b) fraternity without equality
(c) equality without fraternity

Chapter 9

The Family

OVER THE CENTURIES the systems of caste and hereditary occupations helped the villages develop a highly complex, yet stable and orderly society. At the same time, the individual family all over the subcontinent also developed a complicated set of rules. These governed the relationships in the *joint family* — all the people living in one house or courtyard.

Ramiah, a boy of 18, lives in the Indian city of Hyderabad. His father owns a clothing store, has a good income and a house of 10 large rooms. Twelve people live in the house — Ramiah, his parents, his married brother with his wife and three children, his two sisters, a widowed aunt, and a widowed grandmother. Such a household, known as a joint family, is common in the subcontinent. When Ramiah himself marries he will be expected to bring his bride to live in the house of his father. He would not move into an apartment of his own unless there were no room in his father's house.

A joint family: three generations of the Nakti family living together under one roof.

Kamala is a village girl from a poor family. The house in which she lives consists of only two small rooms and a courtyard. But it is shared by herself, her parents, a married brother, his wife and two-year-old son, and an old uncle. When Kamala marries she will go to the household of her husband's father to live. Only in very rare instances do newly married village couples establish a household of their own.

Separate households are set up, however, when sons have many children of their own and need more living space. Sometimes a particularly serious family quarrel leaves no alternative except to break up the family home.

The joint family offers security to the individual. All income is pooled, all food shared. Every person in the joint family is sure that, no matter how hard the

145

times, there is always a place to live and a share of the available food. No household, particularly in the villages, would refuse to accept an additional relative in its courtyard. Nor would any son refuse to care for needy parents in their old age, no matter how little he had or how large his own family was.

Today the joint family system has another "advantage." It enables young married men to work in the cities while their families are cared for in their father's household. Many men live and work in the cities for years, saving their money, before sending for their families.

The system also has "disadvantages." Any family would feel disgraced if one of its members were actually homeless. So it offers him shelter but it won't necessarily encourage him to strike out on his own. Many young men, knowing that their basic needs will be met, are not eager to look for work. Another disadvantage is that when so many people live in close quarters, there is no privacy.

The head of the joint family is almost always the oldest man in the household. His word is law, his position unchallenged. He spends most of his day talking over family affairs with his sons, discussing and supervising farm or business activities, and receiving visitors on his veranda or in the courtyard. This pattern most often occurs in the villages and only if the household head does not have to work in the fields. But even in the cities he makes the final decision on any important family matter, and his advice is sought on all problems.

The head of the household demands and gets the greatest respect from his family. His sons may be well educated, prosperous, and living in the city; he may be illiterate and living in a village. Yet they will bow low and touch his feet as a sign of respect and honor. When Indians say hello or good-bye to their fathers, they hold their palms together so that the tips of the fingers are at the level of the forehead. This is a sign of the special respect due a parent. In an ordinary Indian greeting, the fingertips are at the level of the chin.

In many villages the head of the household is held in such respect or fear that the younger wives of his sons dare not speak to someone else in his presence. Nor would they even dare address him directly unless he first talks to them. This does not mean that the head of the household is regarded as a tyrant. Rather, his years are believed to have given him the wisdom and experience to make the right decisions.

The oldest woman in the courtyard has a similar position of authority. She is usually the wife of the head of the household. If his wife is dead, then the wife of his eldest son takes over. She has complete charge of all the household work — cooking, cleaning, washing, caring for the children. She may not do much of the work herself, but she closely supervises the work of the younger women, making sure that the household runs in an orderly fashion.

The wives of her sons are expected to obey her and to master all the details of running the household. They prepare for the day when they themselves will assume a position of responsibility. She is frequently critical of their performance. They may complain to

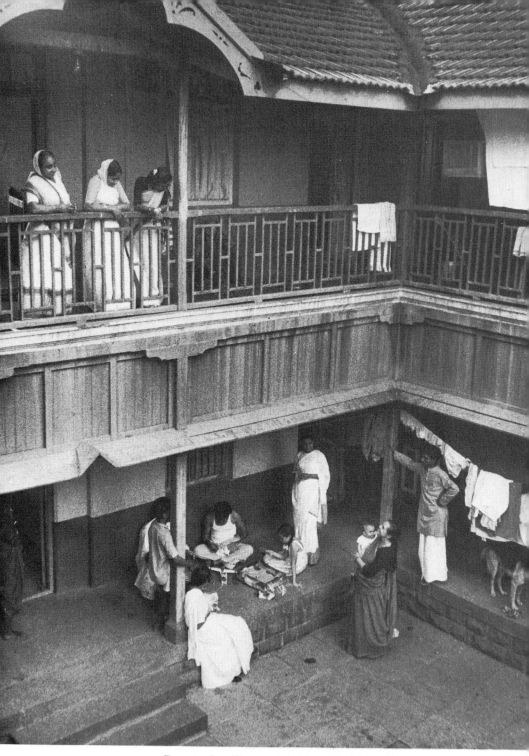

*Day-to-day life in a joint household revolves
around the courtyard. Here, all the adults in the
family gather to do their chores and gossip.*

their husbands, but there is no remedy except to move to another courtyard.

Among the most orthodox families, a man is scolded by his mother if she sees him talk to his wife during the day. The wife herself is scolded for neglecting her duties or for laziness. Young wives have little status in a village household until they give birth to a son. Only then are they really regarded as members of the family.

A modern Indian mother-in-law is usually not a tyrant. She is really interested in the welfare of the entire family group. Moreover, in the cities, mothers-in-law do not often have the authority they do in the villages, even though they are still given great respect by their sons' wives.

As more young men and women of the subcontinent become better educated and move closer to the modern world, they reject some of the traditional family relationships. Sons, for instance, are insisting that they be allowed to set up their own households when they marry. Wives are demanding that they — not their mothers-in-law — make the decisions about their own family life.

At the same time, many of the traditional rules of family behavior are still observed, especially in the villages. For instance, most village women, and many in the cities as well, always walk on the left side of their husbands. The left is considered inferior to the right, symbolizing the supposedly inferior position of the women. (In some areas, however, the women walk on the right.) The women also walk several paces behind their husbands as a mark of respect.

In the villages, when a husband and wife walk together, it is the woman who carries the bundles on her head and the baby on her hip. The husband may carry nothing at all. For the husband to carry the bundles or the baby when he is with his wife would be contrary to custom. It would also lower his status and social standing. The other men would laugh at him for being dominated by a woman.

In most villages and many cities, a woman does not normally join her husband and his guest in talk. Sometimes, when a male guest is in the courtyard, the woman stands half hidden in the doorway of an interior room. She may even keep herself completely out of sight as long as the guest remains. When the

Pakistani women in purdah *wear tentlike cloth called* burqa *over their heads whenever they leave home — which they do rarely, and only with husband's permission. These Karachi women have left homes to be tested for tuberculosis.*

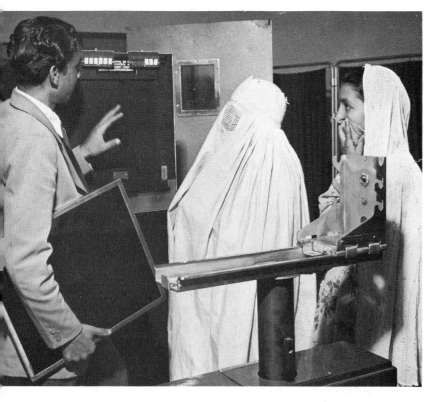

guest is offered tea, the wife prepares it, but it is usually served by her husband. In many regions, custom forbids a wife to serve any male except her husband or members of her family group.

The most extreme form of separation of women from all men except those of their own household occurs in orthodox Moslem families in Pakistan. This seclusion of women is known as *purdah,** which means "curtain." The women who observe strict purdah go into the street only rarely. Before they go out, they must ask permission of their husbands. When they appear outside their homes, they are completely covered by a white or black tent-like cloth known as a *burqa.** A veil completely covers their face.

Some Moslem men regard it as a sign of their own high status and wealth if their wives observe purdah. It means that the man is rich enough to have servants go out into the streets and do all the things his wife would otherwise have to do. Among strict purdah-observing families, women cannot have jobs, go to college, or have any social contacts except with women of other purdah-observing families. At home a woman does not wear the burqa. However, if an unrelated male comes to visit her husband or any other member of her family, she instantly disappears.

Many in Pakistan do not observe purdah. Among poor families, the women must work in the fields and appear in the streets as part of their normal activities. They could not do their work in a burqa or avoid the presence of men. Nor is purdah observed by the families of many government officials, businessmen, and others who want Pakistan to move more quickly into the modern world. Many girls now go to the universities. They, too, do not observe purdah.

Like many of the other old traditions, purdah is slowly giving way to the demands of modern times.

Double-check

Review

1. What is a joint family?

2. When Kamala marries, where will she go to live?

3. Who is almost always the head of the joint family?

4. When Indians say hello or good-bye to their father, what do they do?

5. What does *purdah* mean in English?

Discussion

1. Who is usually the head of a typical American household? Is it "almost always the oldest man in the household"? Would your grandfather automatically be the leader of the household if he lived with your family? How might a typical American family differ from a typical subcontinent family in this regard? Who do you think *should* be the "head" of a household? Why?

2. What are some advantages of living in a joint family household? What are some advantages of living in a nuclear family household? What are some disadvantages of each way of life? Which would you prefer? Why? Which type do you think will be the most common in the future in the U.S.? On the subcontinent? Give reasons for your answers.

3. How do you feel about *purdah?* How would you argue in favor of such a system? How would you argue against it? Do you feel women and men should be equal in society? Why, or why not?

Activities

1. Several students might research different ways of showing respect to people in different societies. They could then illustrate these practices for display on a bulletin board or demonstrate them in front of the class.

2. Several students might role-play a discussion between elderly people from the U.S. and elderly people from the subcontinent about the different attitudes toward the elderly in the two societies. The discussion might focus on how each "elderly person" feels about his or her place in society, and why each person feels the attitudes toward the elderly developed as they did in his or her society.

3. Students might research and report on why, in many societies, the left side and left-handedness are considered "inferior" to the right side and right-handedness, and different societies' customs that show this bias.

Skills

POPULATION OF INDIA, 1980

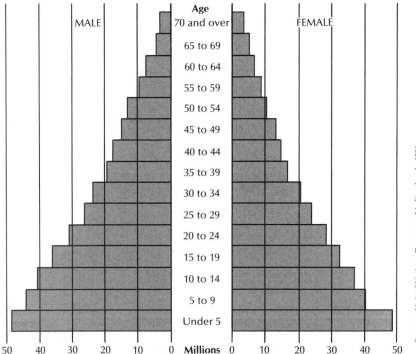

Source: United Nations Demographic Yearbook, 1981

Use the bar graph above and information in Chapter 9 to answer the following questions.

1. What do the numbers down the middle represent? The numbers at the bottom?

2. What does a glance at this graph reveal about the population of India?

3. Which age group includes the largest number of males and females?

4. About how many women in India are 30-34 years old?

5. Who is likely to get more respect in India, a man in the group that includes less than five million Indians, or a man in the group that includes about 25 million Indians? Why?

153

Chapter 10

Marriage: The Most Important Ceremony

FIRST CAME THE BLAST of a trumpet that pierced the darkness, then the steady pounding of drums. A procession of men holding lights above their heads moved down the street. Behind the lights were a dozen dancers, men and women swaying to express their happiness. Behind them was a cluster of about 30 people, and in their midst was the bride-to-be.

The Hindu girl was 17. She was dressed in a silk robe of brilliant green, and her hair, first sprinkled with rose water, was covered with orange blossoms. Pieces of jewelry were pinned to her hair. Her arms were covered with bracelets, no two alike, from wrist to elbow. Her ankles jingled with more bracelets. Silver rings were on her toes. She wore a heavy nose ring of gold, and a sparkling pendant with a ruby in its middle hung over her forehead. Around her neck and waist were chains of gold.

Eyes cast down, a shy smile on her face, she was going to the house of an uncle. There she would receive presents from her future husband's family, and her own relatives would give them presents in return. Then, for an hour or more, female members of

154

both families would sing songs of sorrow and joy. (Usually, however, relatives go to the future bride's home.)

In one house where a wedding ceremony was to be held, a large brightly striped canopy was spread above the lawn in front of the house. Hundreds of colored lights, somewhat like the Christmas tree variety, were strung up on trees, bushes, and the canopy. On the lawn, food tables were set up and chairs put out.

Now the hour had come for the arrival of the groom. The bride looked out nervously through a window. Once again the sound of trumpets and drums was heard. This time it signaled the approach of the groom. Preceded by dancers, he was riding a splendid white horse decorated with gold leaf and jewels. The groom was dressed in white silk, turbaned and bejeweled like a maharajah. He wore a crown on his head and rings on his fingers, and the jewels on his silken coat gleamed.

As he dismounted, his bride came forward from the house, threw a handful of rice at his crown, and slipped a garland of red roses around his neck. Then she ran quickly back to the house. Even though they were soon to be married, it was the very first time the two had seen each other.

Soon it was time for the ceremony to begin. A small sacred fire had been lit on a platform in the middle of the lawn. The bride and groom sat opposite each other, the bride's face covered by a heavy white veil. The groom repeated after a priest that he would always treat his wife well, and the bride repeated vows of obedience. Then the priest fastened the end of a piece of linen to the bridegroom's coat and the other end to the bride's dress. A long series of sacred verses were chanted. From time to time, relatives of

*A Hindu wedding in Bombay. Groom, in elaborate
jeweled headdress, and bride receive food to
symbolize hopes for wealth and many children.*

the young couple sprinkled them with scented water.

Finally the bride and groom walked slowly around the sacred fire seven times. As they did so, more songs were sung. When the seven trips had been completed, the young couple was officially married. The ceremony had lasted more than two hours.

It was now time for the feasting to begin. Because the bride's father was relatively wealthy, the celebration lasted two days. Some weddings may last a week. For the father of the bride, the wedding is more than

156

the celebration of a happy occasion. A wedding represents the successful conclusion of a long and careful campaign to find the best possible husband for his daughter.

Throughout the subcontinent, among Moslems and Buddhists as well as Hindus, it is the parents who arrange the marriage. The young people involved have little to do with it. There are many reasons for this. In the past, some marriages were regarded primarily as a means of creating favorable new ties between families of the same caste or subcaste. Marriage was therefore a matter for the heads of households to arrange.

A more modern explanation for arranged marriages is that young girls and boys do not have much social contact with one another. Parents thus feel their children are not experienced in judging others and that it would therefore be wrong to let them choose their lifetime partners. The parents, it is thought, can make much wiser choices.

Although there is now some resistance to this method, most young people on the subcontinent accept the mate chosen for them by their parents. As for love, the belief is that it should come after marriage, not before.

Sharan is a 24-year-old Indian woman married and the mother of two children. Her husband was chosen for her by her parents. She saw him only once, for about 30 minutes, before they were married. Did she think arranged marriages were good? Absolutely, she answered. In fact, she was astonished when told that in the United States most young people choose their own mates. Perhaps, she said that's why there are so many divorces in the United States. On the subcontinent there are very few.

Until she was 12, Sharan played with all the

neighborhood children, both boys and girls. When she became a teenager, however, rigid custom confined her strictly to the company of girls. Until her marriage at 18, she had practically no contact with boys. She never went to a party with boys, never had a date. Even though her school was co-ed, she rarely talked to boys. All her girl friends grew up in the same way.

When Sharan was 16, her father thought it time to look for a suitable husband for her. It is always the parents of the girl who must search for a mate, never the parents of a boy. Among Hindus he must be of the same caste. Sharan wanted to go to a university and also had considerable talent in classical Indian dancing. So her future husband had to be a university student or graduate who appreciated the fine arts.

Since Sharan's father was prosperous, his daughter's husband also had to be from a well-to-do family. Finally, her father considered the personality of his daughter and the type of person he thought best for her. All this was decided after long conversations between Sharan's parents over a period of months.

When the picture of a prospective husband for his daughter had taken clear shape, Sharan's father informed relatives and a few friends that he was looking for a husband for his daughter. The father was aware that he might not find a young man who met all his qualifications. But he was determined not to settle for anyone who did not come up to his general expectations.

In due course, names of possible candidates began to crop up. Some were rejected immediately. One was regarded as not too intelligent. Another came from a family which had a reputation for being quarrelsome. Finally, one boy was mentioned who seemed to have many of the desired qualities.

**≈§ Throughout the subcontinent
... it is the parents who
arrange the marriage.
The young people involved
have little to do with it.**

One day Sharan's father invited the boy's father to
lunch. During the meal he mentioned that his daughter, a young woman now, would make an excellent
match for a suitable boy. The man understood at
once. He was happy that Sharan's father had ap-
proached him because he regarded Sharan as a good
match for his son.

During this time another crucial step was taken.
An astrologer closely studied the horoscopes of
Sharan and the boy. Millions of people on the
subcontinent will not consider any important undertaking without first consulting an astrologer. When a
child is born, his parents have his horoscope cast and
written out, sometimes in great detail. This information is always taken into account by an astrologer
when consulted.

The astrologer, according to his own formula, studied the position of the stars and planets at the time
each of the two was born and decided that the signs
pointed to a happy and fruitful marriage. He also
specified the month, day, and even the hour the marriage should take place. The date and time would be
when the stars, he said, were in the most favorable
position.

Many people on the subcontinent do not seriously
believe in astrology. But few would feel comfortable
in making marriage arrangements without consulting
an astrologer. And what would the fathers have done
if the astrologer had declared that the stars of the two

~§ Sharan saw her husband only once, for about 30 minutes , before they were married.... She was astonished when told that in the United States most young people choose their own mates.

young people conflicted and a marriage was undesirable? Well, perhaps the astrologer would have been asked to search the stars more deeply and this time come up with a favorable answer. Marriage arrangements have been broken off because an astrologer insisted that the stars of the two people conflicted.

The two men now had a basis for further discussion. At a second meeting a *dowry* — that is, the gifts Sharan's father would give the couple — was discussed. Very often this is a crucial part of the marriage arrangement. If a satisfactory dowry cannot be agreed upon, the two families will break off talks. At this point Sharan's father suggested he would finance graduate studies abroad for his prospective son-in-law, a medical student. He also spoke about later establishing a doctor's office for him. All this would be in addition to the jewelry and clothing that Sharan's father was prepared to give her at the time of the wedding.

As talks between the two families went on, Sharan's father invited the boy and his family to his own home for further discussion. When they came, Sharan saw for the first time the boy who already was virtually chosen as her husband. The two young people did not speak to each other, but the boy's parents asked her some polite questions about herself. Her father asked the boy similar questions. It was the only time the two saw each other before their marriage, the only time they heard each other's voices.

Asked what she thought at the time, Sharan said, "Of course, I felt terribly shy during that meeting. I did not dare to look at Krishna, my future husband. I didn't know what to say or do. All I thought was that if my parents had chosen this boy for me, then he must be someone very good. And, as it turned out, I think they made the best possible choice."

In the aftermath of independence in 1947, long smoldering hatred between Moslem and Hindu broke out into massive violence. Above passer-by steps around corpse in Delhi street.

INDEPENDENCE AND PARTITION

AT THE END OF THE 19TH CENTURY, the great majority of members of the new Indian National Congress were Hindu. Moslems felt that the Congress did not fairly represent their own aspirations. Thus in 1906 they formed the Moslem League. One of its first leaders was the Aga Khan, ruler and spiritual head of the Ismaili sect of Moslems. Immensely wealthy, the Aga Khan was also strongly pro-British. Thus, the Moslem League tended to side with Britain, while the Indian National Congress for the most part opposed it.

This opposition took the form of bombs and bullets in the early 1900's. One such riot occurred when the British government decided that the province of Bengal, with a population of 78 million, was too large. The eastern part of Bengal, which had a Moslem majority, was split off and attached to the next-door province of Assam. The Moslems, a minority in Bengal as a whole, were now a majority in the new province of East Bengal and Assam.

To quiet the revolt — and give India a little of what it had been pleading for — the British Parliament passed the Indian Councils Act in 1909. Under it, most of the members of the Indian state legislative councils were to be elected. Hindu voters would elect Hindu members and Moslem voters Moslem members — both in proportion to the numbers in the general population.

India backed Britain wholeheartedly in World War I (1914-18). In an attempt to repay India for its help, Britain passed the Government of India Act in 1919. Its purpose, as the preamble declared, was to provide "for the increasing association of Indians in every branch of the administration and the gradual development of self-governing institutions. . . ." But this was not enough to satisfy the Indians. With Mohandas K. Gandhi as the new leader of the Indian National Congress, they began their campaign of nonviolent protest and civil disobedience. Gradually the Indians won more self-government.

Meanwhile the Moslems were busy. They knew that Indian National Congress power meant power for Hindus, who made up the majority of Indians — and the Moslems were determined not to become swallowed up in the fight for self-rule. In 1934 Mohammed Ali Jinnah* became the Moslem League's head. He protested that his people were being pushed aside by the Hindus. In time he called for a separate Moslem country, to be cut out of Indian territory. The new country, called Pakistan, would consist of mostly Moslem regions in the northeast (now Bangladesh, see page 207) and northwest. The two regions would be separated by almost a thousand miles of India.

World War II (1939-45) intervened. Britain at first stood alone against the Nazi German air assault. When Britain promised it would grant independence to India if it won the war, the Indian people supported Britain with soldiers and supplies. Japan, Nazi Germany's Axis partner, conquered many of India's Southeast Asia neighbors, but India itself was not attacked.

In 1947 India was granted independence, and Pakistan was set up as a nation in its own right. Both joined the British Commonwealth of Nations.

As India and Pakistan claimed their freedom, the long smoldering hatred between Hindus and Moslems burst into flames. A mass slaughter occurred as many Moslems in India moved to Pakistan, and Hindus in Pakistan moved to India — perhaps 12 million people in all making the shift. Moslems and Hindus fought each other, with an explosive fury. Countless numbers on both sides were slain; estimates range from 100,000 to more than a million. The killing did not cease until the migration was over.

There has been little large-scale religious violence between Hindus and Moslems in recent years. But neither has there been any real friendship between the religious groups. Gandhi's dream of uniting the two peoples still remains just a dream.

Double-check

Review

1. Throughout the subcontinent, among Moslems and Buddhists as well as Hindus, who arranges the marriage?

2. Millions of people on the subcontinent will not consider any important undertaking without first consulting whom?

3. In Sharan's marriage arrangement, what is a dowry?

4. According to the preamble of the Government of India Act in 1919, what was the act's purpose?

5. What caused the Indian people to support Britain during World War II?

Discussion

1. What are some advantages and disadvantages of arranged marriages? In our society, what role do parents usually have in the selection of a mate for their children? Should they have more or less of a role, in your opinion? What role should romantic love play in marriage? Why?

2. What factors do you think account for a higher divorce rate in the United States than on the subcontinent? From what you know of the culture of the subcontinent, what factors other than arranged marriages might help keep the divorce rate on the subcontinent low?

3. Does it make sense to segregate girls and boys at the high school level? Why do you think public schools in the U.S. are coeducational? What, if anything, does this difference between Indian and American schools suggest about the difference in attitude toward education in the two countries?

Activities

1. Some students might prepare a bulletin board display of different marriage customs around the world — from the engagement to the marriage ceremony itself, including information on special clothes, rituals, foods, etc.

2. A science teacher or scientist might be invited to class to discuss the question "Is there a scientific basis to astrology?"

3. Some students might research and report on the Indian constitution and the organization of the Indian government, comparing it with the Constitution and the government of the U.S.

Skills

LIFE EXPECTANCY FOR INDIANS

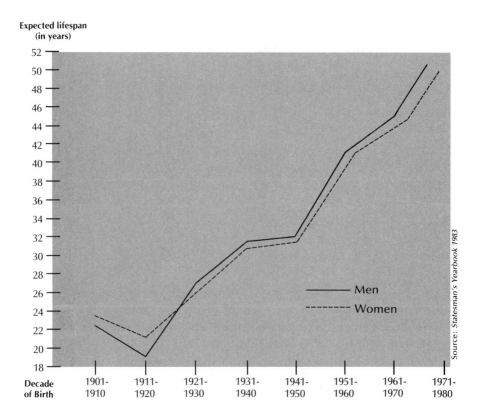

Expected lifespan (in years) / Decade of Birth

Source: Statesman's Yearbook 1983

Use the line graph above and information in Chapter 10 to answer the following questions.

1. What do the numbers on the left of the graph represent?

2. What trend is made clear by a quick glance at this graph?

3. Indian women born during what decades could expect to live longer than men?

4. In India, which group generally seems to live longest, men or women? Give a reason for your answer.

5. An Indian man born on the day Mohammed Ali Jinnah became head of the Moslem League might be expected to die in what year?

Chapter 11

Country Weddings

MARRIAGE ARRANGEMENTS THROUGHOUT the subcontinent do not always follow the same pattern. If anything, the art and business of arranging a marriage is even more complicated in the village than in the city. The head of a household may feel his family disgraced if he has an unmarried daughter. He also faces economic hardship. An unmarried daughter means an extra person to support.

He may even find that his sons have more difficulty in attracting marriage offers. Fathers of young girls might not like the idea of their daughter moving into a household with unmarried women. The reason for this (and it is not entirely without foundation) is that the unmarried daughters might be favored by their mother. The bride who has just moved in might be made to do more than her fair share of the household work.

Villagers who travel are often asked to look for suitable husbands. Barbers are particularly useful matchmakers. In the days before newspapers they

The girl at left is a mother — and that's her daughter at right. Child marriage, although now less frequent, still exists on subcontinent.

were the great transmitters of news and gossip. Even today, as they perform their work, they notice which eligible young men are in good physical shape and which ones have defects. A young man in less than perfect health is not necessarily ruled out. Rather, the father of such a young man may be willing to settle for a less expensive dowry. This is an important consideration for a poor man or one who has several daughters to marry.

After the barber or any other go-between reports on a likely prospect, the girl's father inquires about the boy's family. If the answers seem satisfactory, the girl's father and several male members of his family may travel to the boy's village to begin negotiations. Custom prescribes exactly what kind of presents shall

168

> ⊷§ **Marriage arrangements may
> be made when the girl is only
> 12 or so.... Sometimes, however,
> marriages actually occur
> among children under 10.**

be exchanged at this point and all the other stages of the negotiations. At one point, there may be an exchange of coconuts, believed to be a good-luck omen. If the questions of dowry and horoscopes can be settled satisfactorily, a bargain is concluded and the young people are engaged.

Marriage arrangements may be made when the girl is only 12 or so, though the actual marriage will not take place until several years later. Sometimes, however, marriages actually occur among children under 10. After the marriage ceremony, the young husband goes back to live in his own village, and his bride does not join him for some years.

It sometimes happens that a girl married at eight is a widow at 12. This puts her in a difficult position. It is not easy for fathers of young widows to find second husbands for their daughters. The practice of child marriage is, however, becoming less frequent on the subcontinent and is now technically against the law. It is usually followed only in the poorest and most isolated regions.

A wedding is always an expensive affair for the father of the bride. The dowry he provides must be valuable enough to satisfy the father of the groom. This is not a matter of greed but of economics. Since the boy will have to support the girl for the rest of her life, it is thought that the girl, through her father, should contribute a share to the marriage.

The father of the bride is also obliged to give

presents to many of the groom's family. In addition, he must pay for the wedding feast. It is not unusual for the expense to equal three or four years of a man's earnings. Usually the father of the bride, unless he is wealthy, must go deeply into debt. If he has four or five daughters, he is resigned to a lifetime of debt. Yet he would have it no other way. In the villages, it is particularly important that he promise a big wedding and a big dowry — or else his daughter may not be acceptable to the family he approaches.

Marriage among Indians, Gandhi wrote, "is no simple matter. The parents of the bride and bridegroom often bring themselves to ruin over it. They waste their substance, they waste their time. Months are taken up over the preparations — in making clothes and ornaments and in preparing budgets for dinners. Each tries to outdo the other in the number and variety of courses to be prepared. Women, whether they have a voice or not, sing themselves hoarse, even get ill, and disturb the peace of their neighbors. These in their turn quietly put up with all the turmoil and bustle, all the dirt and filth representing the remains of feasts, because they know that a time will come when they also will be behaving in the same manner."

Many people on the subcontinent would agree with Gandhi's criticisms. Some young men, for instance, now refuse to accept a dowry. These are usually young men from prosperous families who do not really need the added wealth a dowry would bring. Nevertheless, the number of people who would change the marriage customs is still small.

For most, marriage is still the most important ceremony in life. It is vital because it preserves the traditional Indian family unit. And family unity on the subcontinent is prized above all else.

Double-check

Review

1. Why doesn't the father of a young bride like the idea of his daughter moving into a household with unmarried women in it?

2. Why are barbers particularly useful matchmakers?

3. If the questions of dowry and horoscopes can be settled satisfactorily, what happens?

4. Among children under 10, what happens after the marriage ceremony?

5. Why is marriage for most people on the subcontinent the most important ceremony in their lives?

Discussion

1. In your opinion, what is the best age at which people should marry? Why? Why do you think child marriages are against the law in the U.S.? Why do you think child marriages take place in India only in the poorest and most isolated regions?

2. What is your reaction to the pressure placed on the father of the bride in India to give a huge dowry and huge wedding? Does this seem fair? Is there this kind of pressure on the bride's family in the U.S.? Should there be? Give examples to support your answers.

3. Why are people sometimes reluctant to change customs even if the customs seem outdated or useless? What are some customs in our society that you consider outdated or useless, but which still are carried on? Why do you think these customs survive? Can you think of any reason why they should?

Activities

1. Some students might pretend to be Mohandas Gandhi writing a letter to his daughter in response to her request that her father give her a big traditional wedding. Other students might role-play a conversation between Gandhi and his daughter on the subject of big weddings.

2. Some students might research and report to the class on the role of the matchmaker in various societies. They could then lead a class discussion on what types of matchmakers there are in U.S. society.

3. Some students might collect, or draw, symbols of good luck from different countries and then prepare a bulletin board display of the objects or of their drawings.

171

Skills

PER CENT DISTRIBUTION OF WOMEN
BY MARITAL STATUS, 1981

Age	Single	Married	Widowed	Divorced or or Separated
All women 10 to 49 years	27.9	66.5	4.5	1.1
10 to 14	89.3	10.6	0.1	0
15 to 19	47.2	51.9	0.3	0.6
20 to 24	11.6	87.5	0.6	0.3
25 to 29	6.2	91.8	1.3	0.7
30 to 34	3.4	92.8	2.9	0.9
35 to 39	1.0	94.6	3.5	0.9
40 to 44	.7	85.2	14.0	1.1
45 to 49	.3	79.7	18.9	1.1

Source: Indian Government Census Bureau

Use the table above and information in Chapter 11 to answer the following questions.

1. In 1981, what percentage of Indian women between the ages of 10 and 49 were married?

2. By what age is more than half the female population of India married?

3. According to these figures, between what ages do most Indian women get married?

4. Judging from these figures, would you expect that more or less than 79.7 per cent of Indian women over the age of 49 were married?

5. This table gives statistics for 1981. Would it be safe to guess than in 1990 more or less than 11.5 per cent of Indian girls between 10 and 14 were married? Why?

Chapter 12

Food and Clothing

IT WAS SUNDAY AFTERNOON and lunch was being served at the home of the Chopra family in a north Indian city. The first course was a cabbage soup with rice and pieces of tomato. Next, a steaming mound of boiled rice was placed on the table. Around the rice were bowls holding a variety of vegetables and sauces.

One bowl contained small pieces of mutton, tomatoes, onions, garlic, and salt. This was mutton curry. Another bowl had a sauce made of finely shredded pieces of coconut, ground-up chilies (red pepper), and salt. This was coconut curry.

Sometimes the Chopra family has chicken curry, another favorite. Hundreds of different curry dishes can be made by changing the ingredients and the spices. Curries are often sharp and spicy, and with some it is essential for an American or European to have a pitcher of water at hand to put out the fire in the throat. The cook can easily make the dish less spicy if she chooses.

Another bowl on the Chopra table contained sweet tomato chutney, made with tomatoes, cloves, garlic, chilies, ginger, and sugar. There was also a bowl of pickled cauliflower, so sharp that only a touch burned the tongue. Still another bowl held pieces of shrimp in a butter sauce.

Next to the rice was a stack of *chapattis** — round, flat wheat cakes used as bread. To make a chapatti, village women usually grind the wheat into flour right in their courtyard. Some water is added to the flour. The mixture is then worked into a dough, rolled flat, and baked on an iron sheet. The chapatti comes in many variations. It can be fried. It can be made so thin it looks a little like a potato chip. Another kind is filled with vegetables, meat, or any food combination.

The Chopras, like most families on the subcontinent, never use forks or knives. They use the fingertips of the right hand to pick up the food. Pieces of chapatti are used as a scoop or to soak up sauce.

As the final course, the Chopras had homemade yoghurt and fruit — pomegranates,* pineapples, large purple grapes. On week days the family does not have such an elaborate meal. Lunch is one or two vegetables and chapattis, and dinner includes vegetables, a bit of fish or meat, and chapattis. But on Sunday afternoons, the family has its biggest and best meal of the week.

Like all Hindus, the Chopras never eat beef. The cow is considered sacred and is not killed. The Chopras do eat meat from other animals, but many Indians will not eat any kind of meat at all. Some do not even eat fish or eggs or any food containing egg. Even if Indians choose to eat meat other than beef, many cannot afford it. Thus millions of Indians are vegetarians. People in Pakistan, Afghanistan, Bangladesh, and Sri Lanka also cannot afford meat often.

174

The Chopras live in a large city and do their shopping at food stores. But about 80 per cent of the people on the subcontinent seldom buy food at a store and have never bought canned or processed foods of any kind. Almost everything they eat is grown in nearby fields and processed right at home.

For most villagers the major foods are rice or wheat. In the rice regions, people eat rice with each meal. Breakfast might be a bowl of cold rice left over from the previous evening, a glass of buttermilk, and a banana or some other fruit. A typical lunch consists of a bowl of boiled rice, peas, and beans, flavored with peppers and tomatoes. The evening meal consists of more rice, this time flavored with pieces of fish.

On special occasions, pancakes are made from rice powder. The pancakes are eaten plain or stuffed with coconut, potatoes, or vegetables. Rice pudding, sprinkled with raisins, is also popular. Such foods may appear nourishing enough, but people whose diet consists mainly of rice often suffer from a protein shortage. This poses serious health problems, especially for children.

Those used to rice with each meal never seem to tire of it. No matter how large the meal, they go away hungry if they have not had their bowl of rice. By contrast, people in the wheat-growing regions are not happy unless they have chapattis. In fact, people in some of the wheat-growing regions of the subcontinent have refused to eat rice even when faced with near-famine because of crop failures.

Another common food is *dal,** a lentil dish eaten in many regions. Dal is either boiled or fried, flavored with other vegetables, and eaten with potatoes. Usually, a stack of chapattis accompanies a plate of dal. Because it is cheap, this is one of the most common meals eaten by the poorest people.

Seen everywhere on the subcontinent is the *pan wallah** (seller of pan). Pan, a very mild stimulant, is something eaten between or after meals — and many people have it 10, 15, or 20 times a day. On a shiny betel* leaf the pan seller smears a bit of lime paste. He then sprinkles some chopped betel nuts on the leaf, adds a clove, some cardamom, and perhaps other spices, and rolls the leaf into a ball.

This is put into the mouth and chewed. The juices flow, giving the mouth a cool and pleasant feeling. Pan tastes a bit like toothpaste. Experts in the art of chewing pan — it takes years to become an expert — spit out the red juices in one long stream. Spitting pan juice is not regarded as impolite; it is the proper thing to do. The pan juices cause red and black stains on the teeth of many people.

For 80 per cent of the people on the subcontinent, food is rarely plentiful — except perhaps on holidays. There is usually barely enough of it to go around. The average family has the equivalent of only a few dimes a day to spend for food. Meals are simple and often skimpy.

On the subcontinent people wear different types of clothing, depending on the region. When these various types mix on the streets of the large cities, the result is a colorful parade of styles.

The best known piece of clothing on the subcontinent is the *sari,** the dress most women wear. A sari consists of one length of cotton or silk, which comes in an endless variety of colors. The most expensive saris are woven with designs of gold and silver and beautiful decorative patterns. Less costly saris are made of coarse cloth and with no designs.

176

Clothing on the subcontinent is colorful and varied. The sari is widely worn by women all over the subcontinent. At left, woman of Sri Lanka drapes it around her waist. Below, Indian dancer wears silken sari and flowing pants.

In villages, most men,
left, wear dhoti, a strip of cloth
worn around waist. In cities, many
men wear western dress. Some
of the more prosperous, above,
wear tight-fitting Nehru jacket.

Many men on the subcontinent
wear turbans. Above, peasant in Sri Lanka.
Right, Pakistani farmer. Below, Indian Sikhs.

Women of prosperous families have dozens of saris. Most women, however, have only one or two good saris. These are reserved for holiday occasions and are worn only a few times a year.

The sari when worn extends to the ground like an evening gown. It is five or six yards in length and about 45 inches wide. (The sari of orthodox Brahman women is always nine yards long.) The sari is first draped around the waist, then brought under one arm and passed over the opposite shoulder. The end of the cloth may also be used as a shawl to cover the head. With a sari, women wear a blouse.

Draping a sari over the body is a special art. There are dozens of different ways in which a woman can arrange the cloth to fit her mood and the occasion. Often the way in which she wears her sari reveals the area she came from. Women of some regions wear saris of special colors.

Many women on the subcontinent, especially in the north, wear another special kind of clothing. This is a two-piece outfit consisting of tight cotton pants and an upper garment, like a long coat, which comes down to the knees. A silk scarf is usually thrown back over the shoulders. Women wear this when they want more freedom of movement than the sari offers.

These various outfits can be quite elegant. But most women in the subcontinent usually dress much less elaborately. Their everyday clothes consist of inexpensive ankle-length skirts and blouses made of cotton. The colors are usually faded after hundreds of washings. If the women are very poor, their clothes are often ragged.

The clothing of the men is not as distinctive. Men in the cities mainly wear western-type clothing. In the villages, however, most men wear the *dhoti,* a single long piece of cotton cloth, usually white. It is wound around the waist, drawn between the legs, then tucked in at the waist. A white cotton shirt covers the upper half of the body. Some men prefer loose-fitting baggy white trousers and a shirt.

Many prosperous Indians wear the Nehru jacket, popularized by independent India's first prime minister. The Nehru jacket is a tight-fitting garment which buttons right up to the neck. Nehru also wore a small white cotton cap.

Among the most colorful groups of men on the subcontinent are the Sikhs.* The Sikhs never cut their hair or shave off their beards. They believe that to do so would be to weaken themselves. On their heads all Sikhs wear turbans of various colors. Different groups of Sikhs have special ways of tying their turbans.

Most men, like most women, dress very poorly. Some are literally in rags. If they have better clothing, it must be carefully saved. The average man has very little money to buy new clothes. Many of his garments are made at home or by a bazaar tailor.

India's prime minister, in 1980, Indira Gandhi, with picture of her father, Jawaharlal Nehru, free India's first prime minister.

NEHRU: WISE MAN

THE FIRST YEARS OF INDIA'S independence were marred by bloodshed. Muslims and Hindus fought each other on the streets of India's cities. In 1948, Mohandas Gandhi, the nation's greatest spiritual and political leader was assassinated by a Hindu who believed Gandhi had been too tolerant of Muslims.

But the newly formed state was lucky to have Jawaharlal Nehru as its first prime minister. Nehru was a longtime follower of Gandhi who worked to establish democracy in India and to improve living standards.

The son of a wealthy attorney, Jawaharlal Nehru was born in Allahabad, India, in 1889. After attending some of Britain's best schools, Nehru returned to India to practice law. At the same time he took a keen interest in politics.

When Nehru met Mohandas Gandhi, his life was changed forever. He became committed to Gandhi's goal: that India win its freedom, not by armed revolt, but simply by nonviolent resistance.

Nehru was soon Gandhi's good friend and loyal follower. For years both men were in and out of jail for opposing the British. Nehru learned first-hand of the poverty of the Indian people. "Looking at them and their misery, I was filled with shame and sorrow," he said. The people in turn revered him. He became secretary and later president of the Indian National Congress.

When India won independence in 1947, Nehru was named prime minister. He was a forward-looking, active leader. Under him India launched three five-year plans to build up industry and improve people's lives. He asked for—and got— aid from other countries.

In foreign affairs Nehru tried to keep India neutral, siding neither with Communist nations nor the West. Although Nehru often criticized them, both the Soviet Union and the United States considered India a friend. China clashed with India in 1962. But the uncommitted nations in Asia and Africa often took their cues from India in the halls of the United Nations.

Nehru held office until his death in 1964. His daughter,

Indira Gandhi (her husband was not related to the Mahatma), became India's third prime minister in 1967. She continued her father's policy of friendly relations with both the Soviet Union and the West.

In 1975, Mrs. Gandhi came under sharp criticism for briefly breaking with democratic rule. A court found her guilty of corrupt dealing in an election campaign. Her response was to declare a national emergency. Thousands of her opponents were jailed, and the press was censored. She said her actions were necessary to prevent civil war.

Soon afterwards, the Indian parliament passed a bill that legalized the actions Mrs. Gandhi had been convicted of. The Supreme Court of India declared her innocent. However, she lost the next election, and was later jailed for a short period. Despite these troubles, her popularity with millions of Indians never wavered. Many believed her campaign slogan: "Indira is India. India is Indira."

Mrs. Gandhi was elected prime minister once again in 1980. This time her greatest problem was the violence of Sikh terrorists who wanted a separate state. Sikhs are members of a religious sect which unites Hinduism and Islam. Sikhs make up two percent of India's population and most live in the Punjab, a rich and fertile area in the northwest.

In June 1984, Indira Gandhi sent the Indian army to the Golden Temple, the Sikh's holiest shrine. Sikh terrorists were using the temple as a base to attack local Hindus. Between 600 and 1000 Sikhs were killed.

In revenge, two of Mrs. Gandhi's bodyguards assassinated her on October 31, 1984. Her son, Rajiv, was named prime minister several hours later. He had previously been a pilot and a member of the Indian Parliament. His first act was to call for an end to attacks against Sikhs. "This country is not shaken by bullets; India is not broken so easily," Gandhi declared.

For Rajiv Gandhi and the people of India, the future holds many challenges. The greatest among them Gandhi says, "is to get the poor and the weak of India out of the desparate situation they are stuck in."

Prime Minister Indira Gandhi above strolls through a garden with her son Rajiv a short time before her assasination. Below, Rajiv as Prime Minister.

Double-check

Review

1. What are *chapattis?*

2. For most villagers, what are the major foods?

3. What does a *sari* consist of?

4. Who was the first prime minister of independent India?

5. Who changed Nehru's life?

Discussion

1. In your opinion, why did Nehru say he was "filled with shame" about the poverty of his fellow Indians? What responsibility, if any, do you think a wealthy person like Nehru has to help the poor? Give reasons to support your answers.

2. In what ways were Indira Gandhi's political actions similar to her father's? In what ways did they differ? Do you think she chose the best way to deal with Sikh extremists? Give the reasons for your opinion.

3. Some people say that Indians developed the custom of eating the biggest meal of the week on Sunday because of the British custom during the days of colonial rule. Can you think of other Indian customs that were probably influenced by the British? In what way have the customs of the British and other cultures been adopted in the U.S.? Is there such a thing as a purely Indian or purely American custom? Why, or why not?

Activities

1. Some students might research the policies of Rajiv Gandhi toward India, the Sikhs, and other nations.

2. A local nutritionist or home economics teacher might be invited to class to discuss the nutritional value of the typical Indian diets described in this chapter.

3. A committee of students might watch television and read newspapers and magazines for reports on relations between the U.S. and India or other subcontinent countries. Articles and photographs might be displayed on a bulletin board under the appropriate headings.

Skills

SECOND TIME AROUND

Use the political cartoon above and information in Chapter 12 to answer the following questions.

1. Whom does the figure on the left represent?
(a) an Indian dancer   (b) Mohandas Gandhi in women's clothing
(c) Indira Gandhi

2. Whom does the figure on the right represent?
(a) India's people   (b) a drunken sailor   (c) the woman's second husband

3. Why does the figure on the right have a black eye?
(a) He has been abused by Gandhi's policies.
(b) He has fought off other suitors for his bride.
(c) He was injured in the Indian war for independence.

4. What does the main point of this cartoon seem to be?
(a) Indians must be led like cows to better government.
(b) Indians can be happy only in marriage.
(c) Gandhi will continue to abuse Indians even after they reelected her.

4
HINDU MOSLEM AND BUDDHIST

Chapter 13

Hinduism in India

AS THE SUN RISES each morning and the mist slowly clears, an unusual sight comes into view at the city of Varanasi* (also called Benares*), located on India's holiest river, the Ganges. There, three miles of *ghats,** or bathing steps, lead into the water from the 2,000 temples and shrines along the high bank. On some days considered particularly holy, as many as 100,-000 people stand in the water and on the steps. To bathe in the Ganges is considered an act of great piety.

Here and there on the steps are rickety wooden platforms, some covered with canopies or large umbrellas woven of reeds or grass. There holy men sit and talk while their disciples or interested persons listen. The Hindu holy men are considered more as teachers than as clergymen.

Many people apply oil to their bodies. Others concentrate on exercises which twist their bodies into

To bathe in the Ganges is considered an act of great piety.

strange positions. These people are practicing part of the Yoga system of controlling the body. Yoga may be used to train the mind so that one can keep the body free from interfering with the search for self-realization. Yogis (people who practice yoga) can hold their breath for many minutes. Some claim they can stop their heart beat.

All this activity is in preparation for bathing in the purifying river waters. When the sun rises above the horizon and colors the Ganges in a golden light, the people bow low in homage to the sun and then immerse themselves in the water. According to Hinduism, the religion of 84 per cent of all Indians, bathing in a holy river cleanses the body, purifies the soul, and helps prepare it for eventual salvation.

Hindus believe Varanasi to be the earthly home of one of the gods. This is one reason why it is regarded as a holy city. An ancient Indian legend explains why the river Ganges is sacred. According to the story, the Ganges once flowed in a broad path through the heavens. A king wanted to bring the river to Earth to revive his 60,000 sons killed in battle. Finally, after many failures, the river was led to Earth and then to underground regions where the sons of the king lay. And so the Ganges became a holy river, the mother of all Indian waters. Some Indians even drink only bottled Ganges water.

There are many other legends about the Ganges and the gods of Hinduism. Hindu boys and girls grow up hearing these stories many times. One of the popular forms of entertainment is to listen in the evening to these tales related by older villagers or by wandering storytellers.

People come to Varanasi from all over the country. They may have saved for their journey for years. Some pilgrims walk all the way from their homes. Many take special vows before making the trip. Some may decide to fast on certain days of the week. Some may vow to visit a number of Hindu shrines along the way or to give to charity.

When the pilgrims arrive at Varanasi, they usually stay at hostels reserved for people from their region or caste. There are places for Brahmans only, others for South Indians only, still others for people from the north. The morning after arrival, the pilgrims go to the Ganges. After bathing in the river and saying prayers, they visit temples dedicated to their own gods and goddesses.

At the temples, they repeat other prayers, sprinkle flower petals at the feet of the statues of the temple god, and have their foreheads dabbed with colored powder by the temple priest. Usually the pilgrim makes small donations to the priest and to the beggars gathered at the entrance. At sunset crowds of pilgrims gather once again at the river and float earthen lamps out on the water. The Ganges quickly becomes scarlet with the glow. It turns to silver as the moon rises.

If pilgrims wish to win special merit after their visits to Varanasi, they may travel to one of the other sacred spots on the Ganges. There are many such holy places along the river with large crowds bathing at these spots.

Beyond the area of the bathing steps at Varanasi, several log fires are burning. These are where the bodies of dead Hindus, wrapped in white cloth for males and colored cloth for females, are cremated. Many elderly Hindus move to Varanasi, hoping to die and be cremated there so that their ashes can be cast upon the Ganges.

Hindus say the eternal part of a person is the soul and that the body is only its temporary resting place. By cremating the body instead of burying it, some Hindus believe that the soul is freed and able to enter a new body. Other Hindus burn the corpse because that is the custom. They believe the soul has left the body before cremation takes place. Only the bodies of holy men, thought to be in a pure state and free from sin, are not cremated. Instead, they are put directly

Hindu temples are often works of art. These, in Indian state of Madras, look something like wedding cakes. On each layer are hundreds of statues of sacred animals and gods.

into the water to be carried away by the current.

If a Hindu is to be cremated, within hours after the death male members of the family, accompanied by friends and neighbors, carry the body to the burning ghat. The closest male relative, usually the son of the dead person, leads the procession. He is dressed in a white robe and his head has been shaved. After prayers, the body is put on top of the pyre, and the son lights the fire.

Hinduism has many unique features. It does not have one deity or specific prayers which people

193

repeat in the same way and on the same occasions. Instead, Hinduism has hundreds of gods and goddesses, but only a few of them are actually worshipped. All Hindus are free in theory to choose those they wish to worship. Also, they are equally free to choose the way they worship. But of course they are influenced by family tradition and caste customs. Because of its wide choices, Hinduism is sometimes said to be one of the most tolerant of religions.

Many Hindus have in their homes tiny shrines with statues of their personal gods. They pray before them daily, perhaps several times. The village may have a shrine to a different god or goddess. Hindus may also pray there each day. It is not regarded as unusual to believe in several gods and to observe holidays dedicated to them.

It is said that Hinduism is much more than a religion, that it is really an entire way of life and thought. For instance, Hindus believe that every person, because of caste, must perform certain duties. A person born into the subcaste of pottery makers has a duty to be a good pottery maker. If the person is a good pottery maker through life, a major obligation will be fulfilled. But if the person tries to become something else, the obligation will not be fulfilled. That person, in theory, will lead a life of sin.

If people perform their duties well through life, they may be rewarded by being born into a higher caste in the next life. Eventually their souls may reach a state of eternal peace and cease going through the cycle of birth and death. To reach this stage is the highest goal of Hindus.

Double-check

Review

1. What is India's holiest river?

2. According to Hinduism, what does bathing in a holy river do?

3. What is one reason why Varanasi is regarded as a holy city?

4. If pilgrims wish to win special merit after their visits to Varanasi, what do they do?

5. What do Hindus say is the eternal part of a person?

Discussion

1. To what extent do you think we can train ourselves — like yogis — so that our minds will control our bodies? Can we train ourselves to relax and contemplate the beauty of life? In your opinion, how possible and important is "mind over matter"? Give reasons for your answers.

2. Many religions place importance on pilgrimages. For what reasons are pilgrimages valued? Why might pilgrimages create unity and fervor in the religion's followers?

3. What lessons may we learn from legends? Can legends contain "truths" even if the actual events they describe might not have happened? For example, what does the Hindu legend about the Ganges River suggest about the Hindu attitude toward the powers of rivers and kings? What else does it tell us? Does the improbability of the events help or hurt the message? Why?

Activities

1. Some students might examine pictures of Hindu gods and goddesses, and then draw some of these figures for display on a bulletin board. Other students might illustrate the legend about the Ganges River or some other Hindu legend with a series of drawings for the bulletin board display.

2. A practitioner of yoga might be invited to speak to the class and to demonstrate some basic yoga positions and exercises.

3. Some students might research and report on funeral practices in various societies and the reasons behind their development.

RELIGIOUS MAKEUP OF INDIA'S POPULATION

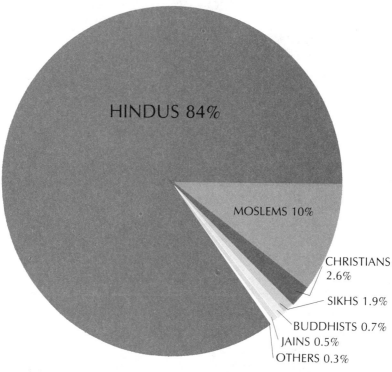

HINDUS 84%

MOSLEMS 10%

CHRISTIANS 2.6%

SIKHS 1.9%

BUDDHISTS 0.7%
JAINS 0.5%
OTHERS 0.3%

Source: *The 1979 World Almanac*

Use the circle graph above and information in Chapter 13 to answer the following questions.

1. What do the numbers in the graph represent?

2. What is made clear by a quick look at this graph about the religious makeup of India?

3. What percentage of India's population practices the second most popular religion?

4. This graph shows that at least how many different religions have followers in India?

5. What percentage of India's population apparently believes that to bathe in the Ganges River is an act of great piety?

Chapter 14

Islam on the Subcontinent

FOR 30 DAYS ALI HAD NOT EATEN or drunk anything between dawn and sunset. During this period his family observed the rule that no one could eat and drink after it was light enough to tell a white thread from a black one. Nor could anyone eat or drink anything during the day until it was impossible to tell white and black threads apart.

The days had been hot and sticky. The temperature usually stood at 100 degrees by noon and it had often gone to 110. Not to be able to take even a sip of water was a major discomfort. This was the 30 days of Ramadan,* when nothing was to pass through the lips between morning and night.

Now Ramadan was over. With thousands of other men, Ali passed through the iron gates into a vast grassy courtyard enclosed by a brick wall. At the far end of the courtyard was a soaring domed mosque* with a roof of deep blue tiles sparkling in the sun. The

*The Peshawar mosque in Pakistan. Unlike
Hindu temples, a mosque is never decorated with
statues. Reason: Islam forbids worship of idols.*

mosque is the temple of people known as Moslems.
Their religion is named Islam, and they call their God
Allah. Ninety-six per cent of the people in Pakistan are
Moslems; 99 per cent in Afghanistan are Moslems;
and about 85 per cent in Bangladesh are Moslems.

Everyone in the courtyard of the mosque was
dressed in white. The worshippers, all men, had taken
off their shoes. They now stood nearly shoulder to
shoulder in neat rows. Each man had a small prayer
rug spread before him.

⋖§ The Koran teaches that every human being is equal in the eyes of Allah. This means that Moslem society is not divided into castes or social groups as in Hindu society.

From one of the four slender towers, or minarets, placed in the four corners of the mosque came a high-pitched, melodious chant. It was the call to prayer. The huge crowd knelt, each man on his prayer rug. Each one then slowly bent his head to the ground. As his forehead touched the ground, he quietly repeated certain prayers. Other prayers were chanted in the kneeling and standing positions.

Soon the prayers were over, and the crowd streamed out of the courtyard. The yearly fast period was officially over, and it was time for feasting and fun. Outside the walls of the mosque was a carnival atmosphere. Men were selling balloons, kites, dolls, other toys. Others had candies for sale. Trained monkeys were performing in one place, trained bears in another. Children pleaded to take a camel ride or to ride on the small carousel. Later, there would be visits to relatives and friends, family members would exchange presents, and everyone would enjoy a big holiday dinner.

Unlike the wide variety of practices and beliefs which Hinduism allows, Islam is very exact in what it teaches. Islam tells the faithful that there is only one supreme being, Allah. Mohammed, who was born in the 6th century in the city of Mecca in the Arabian peninsula, is the last and greatest prophet of Allah.

All Moslems are required to pray five times a day — in the morning, at noon, in the afternoon, at sunset, and at night. When praying, a Moslem must face toward Mecca, a holy city located in Saudi Arabia. A Moslem does not have to be in a mosque to pray. He may put down his prayer rug and worship wherever he is. Friday, however, is the Moslem holy day — much as Sunday is for Christians and Saturday for Jews — and the men usually try to go to a mosque.

Every village in which Moslems live has at least one mosque. These are usually tiny places, but the large cities have mosques with courtyards that can hold many thousands of people. Women do not go to a mosque. They pray in their own home or in their courtyard.

The Koran* is the Bible of Islam. Moslems believe that the words of Allah, as heard by Mohammed, were written down in the Koran. The Koran teaches that there is only one God, Allah. Mohammed is his prophet, as are Abraham, Moses, and Jesus. The Koran predicts a Day of Judgment and outlines codes of behavior for Moslems.

The Koran also says, for example, that women should dress modestly. The Koran teaches the faithful not to eat pork or worship idols. No mosque has a statue of a god or an image of any kind. This is in contrast to Hinduism, with its many statues of the gods.

Another difference between Islam and Hinduism is that the Koran teaches that every human being is equal in the eyes of Allah. This means that Moslem society is not divided into castes or social groups as in Hindu society. In Islam, there is only a single united body of believers in Allah.

Double-check

Review

1. During what period is nothing to pass through the lips of Moslems between morning and night?

2. How many supreme beings does Islam accept?

3. Who is Mohammed believed to be?

4. How often and when are Moslems required to pray?

5. What is the Koran? Whose words are written in it?

Discussion

1. How might the Moslem belief that everyone is equal in the eyes of Allah affect Moslem society? How has the American belief in equality for all affected American society? Do you think a society can have a religious or philosophical belief in equality and yet not have actual equality in its society?

2. Why do you think many religions have a time for fasting? Do you think a fast is a good technique for gaining self-discipline? Why is self-discipline seen as important in many religions?

3. Women play a minor role in Islam, at least in the public sphere. Why do you think this custom developed? Do you think women should be allowed to play a religious role equal with men? Should women be allowed to be leaders of a congregation, for example? Why, or why not? Do you think this will ever change — in Islam or in Christianity?

Activities

1. Someone of the Islamic faith might be invited to speak to the class. A committee of students might prepare questions to ask the speaker about the religious beliefs and practices of Islam, including such subjects as prayer, sex roles, education, diet, and the recent resurgence of Islam in countries of the subcontinent and the Middle East.

2. Some students might read parts of the Koran and choose passages to read to the class for discussion. Other students might list rules of behavior from the Koran and display the list on a bulletin board.

3. Other students might research the influence of the Soviet Union on the subcontinent — focusing on the 1980 Soviet invasion of Afghanistan and on the Moslem nations' responses to it. The students could report to the class on this event and the effect it has had on Soviet relations with Moslem nations.

Skills

MAJOR RELIGIOUS POPULATIONS
OF THE WORLD
(in thousands)

Areas	Christian	Jewish	Moslem	Buddhist	Hindu
North America	260,925	7,611	1,581	330	310
South America	197,642	739	405	240	635
Europe	334,467	4,110	20,201	240	440
Asia	103,741	4,291	378,100	248,770	458,600
Africa	147,400	229	153,220	15	850
Oceania	18,781	74	87	24	325
Totals	1,062,956	17,054	553,594	249,619	461,160

Source: 1985 World Almanac

Use the table above and information in Chapter 14 to answer the following questions.

1. What do the numbers represent?

2. How many Moslems were there in Europe in 1985?

3. Which religion had the greatest number of followers in the world?

4. Which area ranked second in number of Buddhists?

5. How many people in North and South America worshipped Allah in 1985?

Chapter 15

Buddhism in Sri Lanka

THROUGH THE STREETS OF KANDY, once the capital of imperial Sri Lanka, a hundred elephants marched. The tusks of the elephants were sheathed in gold. Their huge bodies were draped with satin cloth, sparkling with jewels and threads of silver. Leading the elephants was a monk in yellow robes. Behind him were dancers, drummers, musicians, singers, acrobats. Men ran along the procession with flaming torches.

At the end of the procession was a single elephant — huge, old, stately — adorned even more spectacularly than the rest. His body seemed almost completely covered with jewels. On his back he carried a shimmering golden casket holding a human tooth. Most of the time, the tooth was guarded as a sacred relic in the Temple of Tooth in Kandy. Now it was paraded through the town as part of one of the most important religious holidays in Sri Lanka.

> **᪗ Buddhism could be called a code for living. It teaches that one must never kill, not even an animal or insect.**

The tooth is said to be that of the Buddha,* a title which means "the enlightened one." About 2,500 years ago lived the man who founded the Buddhist religion, to which most Sri Lankans belong. He was Siddhartha Gautama,* who set out on a lifelong search for wisdom and enlightenment. A prince, he was not satisfied with his life of ease after he realized that so many others lived such hard lives. His father had tried to keep from him the fact that the world was full of suffering. But the young prince saw what the world was like when he went out among the poor, the hungry, and the dying.

The prince wanted to know why there was so much sadness and pain. After years of wandering and meditation, he decided that it was the hunger for the things of the world — wealth, power, comfort, all that people ordinarily regard as desirable — which caused misery. He wanted people to change. He wanted people to stop thinking about themselves and material possessions and demanding the things of the worldly life. He wanted people to think, act, and work with kindness and regard for others. He wanted them to strive for true nobility. Then, he believed, people would be able to find eternal peace, or *nirvana.**

Buddhism, like many other faiths, could be called a code for living. It teaches that one must never kill, not even an animal or insect. People should not desire anything too much, because not having it would cause them unhappiness. Every kind of extreme, either in word or action, should be avoided.

204

If this kind of behavior were faithfully followed, harmony and happiness would result. But they would not be achieved in a single lifetime. Nirvana might not be reached until people had lived through thousands of lives, slowly perfecting themselves a little in each of them. It is said that the Buddha himself went through hundreds of births and deaths before reaching nirvana.

In the quest for nirvana, every young man of the Buddhist faith becomes a monk — most for only a few months, some for years. The monk keeps his head shaved, wears a yellow robe, and begs for his food. He meditates daily, and makes the confession: "I take refuge in the Buddha, I take refuge in the *Dharma** [truth]. I take refuge in the *Sangha* [the order]."

Hinduism, Islam, and Buddhism are three of the world's most important religions. For members of these faiths, religion is one of the most vital parts of their lives. Religion for them is not merely a matter of going to a temple or shrine occasionally. It is a daily experience, one which brings people into close and personal contact with their deity.

The people of the subcontinent celebrate many festivals. Some are related to ancient legends, some to religion, some to the seasons. For instance, *Divali*, the Hindu festival of lights, is said to recall the happy time when an Indian prince and princess, Rama and Sita, returned home after 14 years of exile. During that time they had many strange adventures. Once Sita was seized by the demon king of Sri Lanka but was rescued by Rama, aided by an army of monkeys. This may be why monkeys are regarded as sacred animals by some Indians.

During the Divali season, animals are painted with bright powders. Houses are cleaned and whitewashed. Oil lamps are lit all over the villages and allowed to burn through the night. Doors are left open to let the goddess of wealth enter and bless the household. Candies and presents are passed out to the children.

After the summer months, when the crops are well along, many villages set aside a special day for games. Swings are hung on the trees; young men hold wrestling matches; children have races; recent brides receive gifts from relatives. At the end of the day, everyone goes home for a holiday meal.

One of the most spectacular of all celebrations occurs in Sri Lanka. At this festival, drums beat a fast rhythm, and dancers swiftly spin out of the darkness into a fire-lit square. Their chests and arms have been rubbed with sacred ashes and their bodies are gray. Faster and faster they dance, closer and closer to a long bed of burning coals glowing in the square. Then, in an electrifying moment, one of the barefoot dancers steps on the coals. The spectators gasp and expect him to leap off, but no! He continues to dance over the entire bed of coals. Others follow him, and some go back over the coals a second and a third time. The heat of the coals has been measured at more than 1,000 degrees, yet none of the dancers seems to get burned feet or even blisters.

How is this possible? One explanation may be that a lifetime of walking barefoot makes the soles of the feet so tough that people can literally walk on fire without being burned. Another explanation may be that the dancers have whipped themselves into such a state that they really do not feel the heat. Whatever the explanation, the fire dancers of Sri Lanka are one of the most exotic wonders of the subcontinent.

BIRTH OF A NATION

POLITICS AND WARS make headlines — big ones sometimes. But in thousands of scattered villages throughout the Indian subcontinent, life goes on, often unmindful of what the headlines are saying.

Occasionally, however, a dispute erupts which penetrates beyond politics to the very way people live. Such a dispute led to the breakup of Pakistan in 1971 and the founding of a new nation: Bangladesh.

The roots of this dispute go back to the decision to tie two pieces of land, a thousand miles apart, into one country, Pakistan (see page 163). More than distance separated East and West Pakistan. Between them rose a wall of differences — from language to values.

In West Pakistan, there is a high regard for practical, level-headed people — business, military, and government leaders, for example. The Bengalis of the East are known to be fierier — both in politics and in their love of song and poetry. Most Westerners speak Urdu; in the East the language is Bengali.

Resenting the West's control of government, many Bengalis had long called for an independent Bengali nation. In March 1971, West Pakistani forces tried to crush the Bengali independence movement. Pakistani troops rampaged through the East, raping, torturing, and murdering Bengalis by the thousands. The leader of the Bengalis, Sheik Mujibur Rahman, was arrested and flown to West Pakistan to stand trial for treason. Millions of Bengalis fled to safety in India.

Soon a full-fledged war broke out between India and Pakistan. It was short, but bloody. Within two weeks, the Pakistani army had surrendered and the Bengalis proclaimed a new nation, Bangladesh ("Bengali Nation").

Sheik Mujibur Rahman, released from a Pakistan jail, returned to a wild welcome in Bangladesh. Millions of Bengali refugees in India returned to their villages.

A new nation had been formed. It was a new name on the map — with all of the subcontinent's old problems of overpopulation, hunger, disease, and poverty.

Double-check

Review

1. What does *Buddha* mean in English?

2. Why was Siddhartha Gautama not satisfied with his life of ease?

3. According to Buddha, what causes human misery?

4. In West Pakistan, there is a high regard for what kind of people?

5. Resenting the West's control of government, many Bengalis had long called for what?

Discussion

1. Do you agree with Gautama that the hunger for wealth, power, and comfort has caused human misery? Why, or why not?

2. What problems might result if people *never* killed anything? How can we justify killing anything? Do you agree with the statement that people must kill in order to live? Why, or why not?

3. There were many cultural differences between East and West Pakistan. How much do you think these differences contributed to the clash between the two regions? Is it possible for people with great cultural differences to live in harmony? How do various ethnic groups in the U.S. manage to get along? What types of problems do different ethnic groups living closely together sometimes encounter? How can these problems be overcome?

Activities

1. Some students might write poems, short stories, or short skits about some aspect of the life of Siddhartha Gautama, and present them to the class.

2. Some students might research and report on several Hindu, Moslem, and Buddhist festivals, comparing them to festivals in other religions or to holidays such as New Year's Eve and Independence Day in the U.S.

3. A Buddhist or a religious scholar might be invited to speak to the class about the development of Buddhism, Buddhist belief in reincarnation, and Buddhist influence on life on the subcontinent.

Skills

THREE MAJOR RELIGIONS

A. HINDUISM   **B.** ISLAM   **C.** BUDDHISM

Use the list of religions above and information in Chapters 13, 14, and 15 to do the following. On a separate sheet of paper, write the number of each statement below. Then next to the number of each statement, write the letter of the religion that the statement refers to.

1. There are hundreds of gods and goddesses.

2. Bathing in the Ganges is a pious act.

3. Every young man must become a monk.

4. Varanasi is the home of a god.

5. Worshippers must pray five times daily.

6. The founder lived about 2,500 years ago.

7. Yoga is practiced to control the body.

8. People must not kill — not even insects.

9. There is a 30-day fast.

10. Worshippers use small prayer rugs.

11. There are no specific prayers.

12. Worshippers face toward Mecca when praying.

13. If a person is good, he or she might be born into a higher caste in the next life.

14. Worshippers strive to reach *nirvana*.

15. The religion of 85 per cent of Bangladesh.

16. *Divali*, festival of lights, is celebrated.

17. Sometimes said to be the most tolerant religion.

18. Worshippers follow "the enlightened one."

19. Worshippers follow Mohammed, said to be Allah's prophet.

20. Founded by Siddhartha Gautama.

21. The Koran is its Bible.

EPILOGUE
A CHANGING AND
CHANGELESS WORLD

UNDERSTANDING THE INDIAN SUBCONTINENT is not
a simple task. Though divided into just five countries, the subcontinent really contains many different
worlds. Some have little or no contact with the others.
Often the gap between the city and the village
amounts to something like the gap between the 20th

and the 16th centuries. Between the factory worker and the farmer often lies an equally wide division.

Science and technology have brought great changes to the subcontinent since the 1950's. Now atomic energy is used to find underground sources of water. And some of the world's biggest dams are producing vast amounts of power for electricity. In the years ahead the electricity will be brought to tens of thousands of villages. Electricity will also enable industry to grow.

On the subcontinent the world's largest canal systems are irrigating millions of acres. Land which gave poor crops is now producing in abundance. Slowly the subcontinent is becoming better able to feed itself. It is making this progress despite the great increases in population each year.

The countries of the subcontinent already play a major role in the world's economy. India is the world's seventh largest steel producer, though it still cannot make enough steel to fill all its own needs. Its factories produce a wide range of manufactured goods — engines and tools, cars and bicycles, bricks and cement, aluminum and plastics. Many of India's products, such as tea, sugar, and spices, are shipped to other countries.

Pakistan has built many factories since the 1950's, and exports large amounts of cotton and tobacco. Afghanistan exports natural gas. Bangladesh produces much of the world's jute, which is used to make burlap.

Sri Lanka has a larger area planted with coconut palm trees than any other country. It is second only to India in tea production. Rubber is another major product of Sri Lanka.

Beneath this developing world, however, lies a world of caste, of tradition, of custom. In this world, people still struggle to get enough food. They still live in small houses made of mud and bamboo. They still suffer from great poverty. Their children still lack educational opportunities.

The people waver between strict observance of traditional ways and interest in modern methods. The subcontinent's leaders want to adopt the latest techniques and bring rapid improvements in living. Yet their people are still influenced by many ancient habits. Impatient to build up industries as quickly as possible, the countries of the subcontinent are slowed down and sometimes blocked by shortages of money and skills. Caught between the new and the old, the people are eager to try the one, but hesitant about giving up the other.

The United States and many other countries, as well as the United Nations, have been helping the subcontinent improve its living conditions. Much of this assistance has been in the form of equipment, skilled technicians, and expert advisers in a wide variety of fields — agriculture, industry, education, health, transportation, communications. Yet this has been only a small part of the total effort. Most of the thrust has come from the countries of the subcontinent themselves.

In the years ahead the Indian subcontinent will be under many additional strains and pressures, particularly as its population continues to shoot upward. What will happen cannot be predicted. Will the subcontinent's determination to better the human condition go on? What will become more important — spiritual values or material progress? Or will both be stressed? Whatever happens, the Indian subcontinent and its people will become increasingly important members of the world community.

Pronunciation Guide

Amritsar — ahm-RIHT-sahr
Anuradhapura — ah-noo-rah-DAH-poo-rah
Aryans — AIR-ree-uhnz

Benares — BEH-nuh-rehs
betel — BEET-'l
Brahman — BRAH-muhn
Buddha — BOO-duh
burqa — BOOR-kuh

Chandni Chowk — CHAHND-nee CHOHK
chapattis — chuh-PAH-teez
charpoy — CHAHR-poi

Dacca — DAHK-uh
dal — DAHL
dharma — DAHR-muh
dhoti — DOH-tee
Dravidians — druh-VIH-dee-uhnz

Mohandas Karamchand Gandhi — moh-HAHN-duhs
    kuh-RAHM-chahnd GAHN-dee
Siddhartha Gautama — sih-DAHR-tuh GOH-tuh-muh
ghats — GAHTS
ghee — GEE
Gopal Krishna Gokhale — goh-PAHL KRIHSH-nuh
    GOH-kuh-lay

Harappa — HAH-ruh-puh
harijans — HAH-rih-jehnz
Himalaya — hih-MAH-lee-yuh
hookah — HOO-kah

Hyderabad — HIGH-druh-bahd

Mohammed Ali Jinnah — moh-HAH-muhd
  ahl-LEE juh-NAH

Koran — KOH-rahn
Kshatriyas — kuh-SHAH-trih-yuhz

Madhya Pradesh — MAH-dyuh pruh-DAYSH
maharaja — mah-huh-RAH-juh
Meerut — MEE-ruht
Mohenjo-Daro — moh-HEHN-joh DAHR-oh
mosque — MAHSK

nawab — nah-WAHB
Jawaharlal Nehru — juh-WAH-hahr-lahl NEH-roo
nirvana — nihr-VAHN-uh

pan wallah — PAHN WAH-luh
pariahs — puh-RIGH-uhz
pomegranates — PAHM-uh-gran-uhts
Punjab — PUHN-jahb
purdah — POOR-duh

Ramadan — RAH-muh-dahn
rupees — ROO-peez

sari — SAH-ree
sepoys — see-POIZ
Shudras — shood-RAHZ
Sikhs — SIHKS
Sri Lanka — sree LAHN-kah
swaraj — swuh-RAHJ

Taj Mahal — TAHZH muh-HUHL
Bal Gangadhar Tilak — BAHL gahn-gah-DAHR
  TEE-luhk

Vaishyas — VIGH-shuhz
Varanasi — vuh-rah-nuh-SEE

Index

*Photograph.

family life, 144–151, 145,*
    148*
farming on subcontinent,
    35–36, 39–41, 49–51
fishing on subcontinent,
    52–53
food, 173–176
France in India, 44

Gandhi, Indira, 182,* 184
Gandhi, Kasturba, 140
Gandhi, Mohandas, 29, 89,
    134, 139–141, 163–164,
    170, 184
Ganges River, 92,* 188,*
    189–192, 190*
geography of subcontinent, 12
ghee, 26
Gokhale, Gopal Krishna,
    87,* 89
Government of India Act,
    163
"Green Revolution," 52–53

Harappa, 28
harijans, 29
Hastings, Warren, 44
Hinduism, 29, 116,* 119,*
    127, 140, 155–156,
    163–164, 174, 189–194,
    188,* 190,* 193,* 205–206
Holland in India, 44
hookah, 32
housing in villages, 24–27
Hume, Allan Octavian,
    88–89
Hyderabad, 57

India, independence of,
    162–164
Indian Councils Act, 163

Indian manufacturers in 19th
    century, 88
Indian mutiny, 65–67, 65,*
    87
Indian National Congress,
    141, 162–164
Indus River civilizations,
    28–29
irrigation, 95*
Islam, 117,* 136–138,
    163–164, 197–200, 198*

Jinnah, Mohammed Ali,
    163–164

Kandy, 203
Karachi, 57
Kashmir, 86
Kshatriyas, 29

Lahore, 57
languages, 16 (map), 17
literacy, 16
Lucknow, 67

Madras, 57, 81, 107*
Markandaya, Kamala, 35–36
Mohenjo Daro, 28
monsoon season, 22, 23
    (map), 35
Moslem League, 162–164

Nectar in a Sieve, 35–36
Nehru, Jawarhalal, 134,
    182–184, 185*
Nepal, 93*
New Delhi, 58
nirvana, 204–205

Pakistan, independence of,
    162–164

pan wallah, 176
Peshawar, 198*
Plassey, Battle of, 44
population of subcontinent
    nations, 12
Portugal in India, 43–44
Porus, 42,* 43
poverty on subcontinent, 12,
    20, 35–38, 70–78, 98,* 99
purdah, 150*

Rahman, Sheik Mujibur, 207
Ramadan, 197–199
Red Fort, 58, 59*

Sanjivayya, Damodaram,
    137*
Sanskrit, 29
saris, 176, 180
Sepoy Rebellion, 65–67, 87
Shudras, 29
Siddhartha Gautama (the

Buddha), 204
Sikhs, 102,* 121,* 179,* 181

Taj Mahal, 58–59, 116*
Tilak, Bal Gangadhar, 87*

Untouchables, 29, 129–131,
    130,* 134–137, 135*

Vaishyas, 29
Varanasi, 92,* 189, 190–198
Victoria, Queen, 87
village government, 32–34
village life on the
    subcontinent, 19–53

weddings and courtship,
    154–161, 156,* 160,*
    167–170
women, role of, 147–151,
    156,* 157–161, 160,*
    167–170